plato
for
everyone

Aviezer Tucker

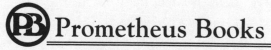

Prometheus Books

59 John Glenn Drive
Amherst, New York 14228–2119

Published 2013 by Prometheus Books

Cover image © 2012 shutterstock
Cover design by Nicole Sommer-Lecht

Inquiries should be addressed to
Prometheus Books
59 John Glenn Drive
Amherst, New York 14228–2119
VOICE: 716–691–0133 • FAX: 716–691–0137
WWW.PROMETHEUSBOOKS.COM

17 16 15 14 13   5 4 3 2 1

Library of Congress Cataloging-in-Publication Data

Tucker, Aviezer, 1965–
    [Works, Selections]
    Plato for everyone / by Aviezer Tucker.
        p. cm.
    Includes bibliographical references.
    ISBN 978-1-61614-654-2 (pbk. : alk. paper)
    ISBN 978-1-61614-655-9 (ebook)
    1. Plato. I. Tucker, Aviezer, 1965– II Title.

B395.T83 2013
184—dc23

2012040648

Printed in the United States of America on acid-free paper

CONTENTS

INTRODUCTION

Subversive! Provocative! Funny! Intellectually stimulating and challenging! Downright annoying! Socrates was anything but irrelevant or boring to the ancient Athenians. Indeed, the Socrates that emerges from Plato's dialogues subversively challenged everything the ordinary Athenian citizen held sacred, within the civic consensus, beyond doubt: their religion and patriotism, the expertise of politicians and other professionals, the established social hierarchy, and their sense of propriety and morality. Whatever else Socrates's contemporaries may have thought of him—and they did execute him eventually—they could not accuse him of being irrelevant.

Something not very pleasant happened to Plato's Socratic dialogues on their way from the Athenian marketplace (the agora) to the twenty-first-century bookstore and classroom. The modern reader and student who does not possess excellent knowledge of classical Greece and its history, culture, religion, art, and literature often misses the subversive and humorous aspects of Plato's dialogues that were obvious to their targeted original readers. Lost in translation, readers often miss much of what the ancient readers would have found poignantly relevant.

Contemporary productions of classical plays and operas frequently transpose the plot and scene to the present to demonstrate that the universal qualities of the classics are independent of any particular historical era or geographical origins. They demonstrate the contemporary relevance of plays and operas that were written for and about different eras. Shakespeare's *Richard the Third* and *Macbeth* often portray contemporary dictatorships and tyrannies, highlighting the universal qualities of self-destructive lust for power that have been more manifest during the twentieth century than perhaps any other period in history. One production of *Romeo and Juliet*, about absolute, tragic love that transcends tribal rivalries and loyalties, was set in contemporary Los Angeles among members of rival street gangs. Its contemporary relevance could be (and perhaps has been) demonstrated whether it were set in Northern Ireland or the West Bank or Rwanda—or any other area of tribal conflict. Beethoven's opera *Fidelio* and Puccini's *Tosca* explore the universal themes of freedom and tyranny. No wonder they have been staged in various historical times and in places where artistic freedom and dissent had to confront political oppression—from a Nazi concentration camp to Maoist China. Mozart's *Don Giovanni* has been set in the South Bronx. I watched Verdi's *Macbeth* in Berlin, where the production took place in the former East Germany, and Wagner's *Meistersinger* in Cologne set in that city and concluding with the construction of the Cologne Opera House itself, opened by West Germany's chancellor, Konrad Adenauer. All these contemporary adaptations of stage classics bring home to the audience the contemporary relevance of their universal themes. They introduce contemporary analogies to past themes, characters, and plots, bringing them home, as it were.

Plato's philosophical dialogues are also classical plays. They explore universal themes that can be manifested in different historical contexts and interpreted and reinterpreted as contemporary and relevant by each generation. I offer here such an interpretation of Plato for our time.

Having discussed Plato's dialogues in English translation with students in several classes, I found that two aspects of the dialogues get in the way of fully appreciating and enjoying them. First, many students have never read a play before. They read novels and short stories, but the format of reading rather than performing or watching a play was unfamiliar. They found the style fragmentary and difficult to follow, and they preferred the natural flow of a story. Second, since the large majority of the students were not familiar with classical Greek civilization, they found many of the cultural and historical references in the dialogues puzzling and distracting. They missed the philosophical essence of the dialogues as they attempted to come to grips with the exotic cultural references. Plato's dialogues are full of humor and repartees between Socrates and his interlocutors, but it is easy to miss them if the reader is not familiar with their cultural context. I explained the jokes in class, but jokes that need to be explained rarely end up being funny. These barriers have nothing to do with the philosophical questions, methods, and contents of the dialogues, which I consider their essential and important aspects. Most people read Plato's dialogues to become familiar with the problems of philosophy, the Socratic method of dealing with them, and Plato's proposed solutions. The classical cultural context is inessential and can even be distracting.

These academic experiences led me to the idea of rewriting some of Plato's dialogues in the form of short stories and moving the scene and plot to the present United States. This kind of pedagogical strategy may offend purists who would rather adhere to teaching translations of the original, but let us not forget that Plato's dialogues used to be taught exclusively in the original Greek. We started teaching Plato in translation only much later. Teaching a contemporary version of Plato's dialogues rewritten as stories would be just one more step in the direction of making Plato more accessible to a wider public without compromising the philosophical essence of the dialogues, the drama, and the humor.

I attempt to refresh Plato's arguments to make them as relevant today as they were two and a half millennia ago. Rather than challenge Athenian mores, civic virtues, and religion, which nobody holds today, I updated the dialogues to challenge and indeed to provoke today's readers by critically examining deeply held but rarely challenged social norms, religious beliefs, and political practices. I attempted to sharpen and retain the subversive cutting edge of Socrates's and Plato's philosophy, which has been blunted over the centuries by the passage of time. The value of the provocation should be, to paraphrase Kant's comment regarding Hume, in waking up the readers from their dogmatic slumber to the challenges and possibilities of philosophy. Whatever other impressions readers may take from this book, they should not remain indifferent or disengaged. Socrates was provocative, and so is this book. I do not expect or even wish the reader to adopt or accept all or most of the arguments and opinions my Socrates presents here. Indeed, I do not agree with everything my Socrates says in this text. I do hope, however, that the reader will learn how to ask questions; how to doubt commonsense, everyday beliefs and assumptions; how to inquire critically; how to be actively curious; how to think like a philosopher; and, eventually, how to experience what is it like to be a philosopher.

I wrote this book thinking of it as the first philosophy book an imaginary reader might pick up at a bookstore or study in an introductory class in college, community college, or high school. The texts are accessible and entertaining without compromising or dumbing down their philosophical contents. I

worked with Benjamin Jowett's classical and literary translations, attempting to preserve the problems, questions, arguments, and attitudes while transposing the sociohistorical
backgrounds and the characters and their contexts. I made no
assumptions about what my reader knows or does not know
about philosophy. This book really is for everyone, irrespective
of background, education, age, gender, religious and political
orientation, taste in music, shoe size, favorite television show,
and zip code. I hope that in addition to nonphilosophers and
beginning philosophers, some advanced and professional
philosophers will read this book, just as people who know
Shakespeare verbatim and are proficient with the critical literature about his plays may want to watch a new production
because they are curious to see a fresh and innovative interpretation of his works.

I present here contemporary interpretations of Plato's
Crito, Meno, Euthyphro, the *Apology,* and *Phaedo.* The first four
are the early "Socratic" dialogues that preserve the historical
Socrates's philosophical practice and opinions—distinct from
Plato's later philosophical developments. The *Phaedo* presents
Plato's version of the death of Socrates. These dialogues are
perhaps the most dramatic of Plato's dialogues in comparison
with the more expository, programmatic ones in which Plato
uses the literary figure of Socrates to expound his theory and
argue against alternative theories. I attempted here to accen-
tuate the drama by shifting the scene and social dilemma from
Athens to philosophically comparable contemporary social
contexts.

The *Crito* considers the obligation of citizens in a democratic state to obey its laws, even when they believe the laws
are unjust. In the original Platonic setting, the dilemma is
whether Socrates should allow his friends to help him escape

prison to avoid execution and go into exile. This is not the kind of dilemma that we usually face these days. A more pertinent dilemma to bring out the moral conflict about obeying unjust but legitimate laws is conscription to serve in a military that is engaged in an unjust war declared by a democratically elected and constitutional government. The conflict between the duty of the citizen in a democratic state to obey its laws and the moral obligation of any human being to abstain from participating in unjust acts is fleshed out in a way that is relevant today in a story about Socrates's decision to accept conscription rather than go into exile in Canada against the background of an unjust war.

The *Meno* examines the meaning of what the Greeks called *arête*, usually translated into English as virtue. However, the Greek meaning of *arête* is much closer to the American slang adjective *cool* than to the Judeo-Christian notion of *virtue*. The result, then, is the first philosophical dialogue about the meaning of *cool*, featuring Socrates and Miles—the coolest college student—during spring break in New York City. As they talk, they discuss the nature of knowledge and learning against the background of contemporary academia, unlike the sophists against whom the historical Socrates debated.

The *Euthyphro* examines piety and ethics through the story of a fanatically conservative Athenian priest who is about to sue his father for murder for having inadvertently caused the death of his slave through exposure after that slave killed another slave. In Athenian eyes, this charge was about as ridiculous as a televangelist seeking to disown and expel his son from his church for having a girlfriend. As in the Platonic original, this dialogue establishes the distinction between philosophy and religion when Socrates asks whether God forbids murder because it is evil or whether murder is evil because God says so.

The *Apology*, Socrates's defense speech at his trial, is a classic of world literature. The particularly Athenian legal and political context is not important today, but the conflict between the uncompromising principled philosopher and the conformist, complacent, and eventually corrupt society is universal. Socrates is probably the first dissident to unintentionally offend society by practicing his philosophy and applying it to question the rationality of expertise and the social hierarchies and norms that are legitimized by it. Our society has made some progress over the years, so we do not prosecute and execute our Socrateses. More often, they lose their jobs and suffer from social ostracism. A relevant contemporary parallel would be if Socrates were a teacher and some of his students' parents accused him of corrupting their children and demanded his dismissal.

The *Phaedo* tells the story of Socrates's last day as he prepares to drink the poison hemlock (this was how the Athenian state executed convicted criminals) and defends his decision to accept the death sentence. He discusses his concept of the immortality of the soul and the theory of ideas, and he demonstrates by example a philosophical indifference rather than fear as he faces death. The eternal questions of how we should live, confronting death, and whether we should shorten our own lives are raised today through the ethical dilemmas that involve euthanasia and the right to die. Accordingly, my adaptation of the dialogue also takes place during Socrates's last day, but he is in a hospice suffering from a chronic disease, decides to die, and justifies his decision.

A few words on my perspective. My interpretation of Plato's dialogues is influenced by my studies as an undergraduate with Professor John Glucker at Tel Aviv University. Glucker's focus on asking what the problem is that Plato attempts to answer as the central issue of each dialogue rather than the answers or doctrines and his interpretative principle that considers Socrates's appeals to myth and mythologies as intentional self-irony that could be read as a declaration of intellectual defeat influenced me most, though of course he is not responsible for what I made of his interpretative principles a quarter century after I was his student. Another totally different influence has been the interpretation of Socrates by the Czech dissident philosopher Jan Patočka, who followed in Socrates's personal footsteps, provoking the communist Czechoslovak regime with his philosophical practice, culminating with cofounding the Charter 77 movement for human rights. Patočka emphasized care for the soul and life in truth as the core philosophical values that confront and offend the state. His own confrontation with finitude and Socratic self-sacrifice are cases of interpretation by example. Readers who are interested in this interesting philosophical and political episode may wish to have a look at my book *The Philosophy and Politics of Czech Dissidence: From Patočka to Havel* (Pittsburgh: Pittsburgh University Press, 2000).

Socratic choices between suffering injustice and participating in committing injustice have not disappeared in the past two and a half millennia. In that respect at least, Socrates's philosophy has lost none of its relevance. Two such choices that were forced on me have influenced my reading of Plato's dialogues and my present interpretation. In 1982 the democratically legitimate government of Israel initiated an unjust war in Lebanon. My generation of Israelis was forced to make a choice similar to the one my Socrates is facing in my rendition of *Crito*: whether to obey the law and suffer injustice or to disobey the law and avoid committing a different type of injustice.

More recently, I was forced to choose between keeping an academic job at Queen's University Belfast at the cost of committing injustices, becoming a secret informer for morally

nihilistic managers against my colleagues, debasing the philosophical education I was offering to students to the level of
bullet points, forging grades irrespective of performance, and
suffering the injustice of being harassed out of my job. You
can read about it in my article "Bully-U: Higher Education and
Central Planning," *Independent Review* 17, no. 1 (2012): 99–119.
This Socratic choice affected my rewriting of the *Apology*.

These personal experiences illustrate the universality of the
themes of Plato's dialogues. They are relevant in most diverse
personal and historical contexts. Indeed, they force themselves
on us whether or not we want to face them. The pivotal, game-
changing episodes in our lives may be described as a series of
Socratic choices.

We can use Socrates as a guide for understanding our
contemporary dilemmas and choices, just as if he were living
among us today. Of course, we can understand our choices
in Socratic terms, without accepting his resolutions of them.
Personally, I rejected Socrates's conclusion in the *Crito* but followed his example in the *Apology*. Still, my conceptualization of
my moral choices was wholly Socratic. If there are things worth
suffering for, justice must be one of them. The head of human
resources at Queen's University Belfast, a brute of a man, told
me, "Don't tell us about Socrates, we already know everything
about him" and then laughed at his own silly joke. But, no, he
knew nothing, absolutely nothing about Socrates, or he would
not have been a moral nihilist. Had he read the dialogues that
inspired this book, he would have understood how utterly futile
was the attempt to force a philosopher to commit injustices at
the threat of suffering from injustices. If this book has one positive effect, I hope it will be to convince some readers that it is
better to suffer injustice than to commit injustice.

IS IT GOOD TO DIE FOR ONE'S COUNTRY?

(After the *Crito*)

The war just dragged on. It was a dumb war. It was also a particularly senseless war. Our democratically elected government chose to start this war. The war was not forced on us. We were not attacked first. Our leaders and their strategic advisers miscalculated, thinking that if they took sides in a local conflict, the side they backed would win. But the calculation of our leaders was wrong. The goals of both sides in that conflict were equally reprehensible; they just wanted to bully, intimidate, rob, and ultimately kill each other. It was a war we could not have won and should not have been involved in in the first place. Meanwhile, the war continued. Conscripted young men were forced to fight in that war whether or not they supported it. Those who refused went into exile or were jailed in military prisons.

By the time Socrates became eligible for conscription, the political question was how to end the war without losing face. The politicians did not want to admit they had been wrong to start the war. They were looking for some face-saving achievement they could use to claim that the war's goals had been realized. They were also afraid that a quick withdrawal would cost our country prestige and its power of deterrence against other potential enemies. To get us out of the war they should not have started in the first place, they felt they had to get us even deeper in that political and military mire.

Socrates, along with the rest of us, opposed the war from its inception. We demonstrated against it. We authored and signed petitions for peace. We campaigned against the ruling parties and voted against them in the elections. But to no avail: they still won the elections. The roaring guns silenced the voice of reason. Some of our friends fled the country to avoid the draft. Others were drafted. Some of them died in battle or returned wounded or maimed. To be sure, the war was becoming increasingly unpopular. Eventually, some government would be forced to end the war one way or the other, to pretend it had achieved something. But until then, the killing would continue.

Young people who had not yet been drafted and who had not left the country were living on borrowed time, waiting to receive their draft notices. When they received their notices, they had to decide whether to obey, to attempt to game the system, to appear to comply but in fact avoid active duty, or to flee the country. When his time came, Socrates was sleeping. We were sitting in the kitchen drinking tea and talking politics. Chris, Socrates's roommate and childhood friend, brought in the morning mail. We all recognized the dreaded envelope from the draft board. Anxiously, we looked for the name on the envelope. It was Socrates's.

Chris entered Socrates's room and sat by the side of his bed. Socrates woke up, opened his eyes, and asked Chris why he was sitting there in the middle of the night. "It is almost noon," answered Chris, smiling tenderly. Socrates sat up in bed and asked Chris how long he had been sitting there. "For a while. I did not want to wake you up."

"Why have you not awakened me, if it is so late?" wondered Socrates.

"I wanted to let you sleep. You looked so peaceful and calm. I sleep so badly. I keep waking up through the night with anxiety and dread, and yet, despite the war and all, you sleep like a neutral Swedish baby who does not expect to ever wear uniforms and carry a gun. I have always admired your calmness in the face of danger and adversity. I wanted it to last for as long as possible, so I let you sleep."

Socrates nodded. "I find people in general are too anxious about things that are unimportant. I reserve my limited worrying capacities to things worth worrying about. Still, you have obviously been waiting here to tell me something. What happened?"

"I am sorry, Socrates. I have to bear sad and painful news. Not just to you but to all your friends. This is particularly sad for me."

"I suppose you picked up the mail as usual. But today is different. Today, I received a letter from the draft board ordering me to present myself to be conscripted into the military, yes? Unpleasant but hardly surprising."

Chris passed the envelope to Socrates in silence. Socrates opened it deliberately but without haste. "In three days," he announced without much emotion. "I dreamt about it last night. In my dream, Lady Liberty, looking like the Statue of Liberty, came to me and told me I will have three days with her. She looked kind of sexy."

Chris laughed and said, "Quite a dream, no doubt, Socrates. Prophetic." He then turned serious. "My dear friend, we talked about this before, but now it has become urgent. Please, I beg you, accept my advice and let me help you escape. You need not worry about me and my friends. We are not afraid of informers or of being prosecuted for helping you leave the country. We will gladly take such risks to save your life. We have helped other conscripts escape before. We have established routes and volunteers who will help you cross the border. This will not cost us much either. A few modest commissions for border guards and immigration lawyers suffice to get conscripts across the border and into safety. If you worry about my own personal expenses, do not. We have wealthy backers who share our cause. They will gladly pay all the expenses of your escape. Do not hesitate and do not worry. It will be easy. There are many places in the world where you will be welcomed and will be able to continue your studies. I have many friends in Toronto, Canada, for example. If you would like to go there, they will protect and help you. In Toronto, nobody will harass or bully you. Quite the opposite, they will value and cherish you. You will feel almost at home there.

"You should not risk and possibly sacrifice your life for nothing, for a stupid and immoral policy enforced by a government that cannot admit it was wrong. It would be total folly on your part to obey this draft order when you have a readily available alternative: to just get the hell out of this country. If you allow yourself to be drafted, you will do their bidding. You are exactly the kind of political dissident—critical of government policies—whom they would love to see dead. They could even use your death in war as an example for others to follow; make you into a martyr for the impossible goals of this war.

"You should also think about your family. What about your parents? Don't they have the right to be taken care of in their old age by their eldest son? Would you not be betraying your obligation to them if you leave them now, let alone if you are killed? What about your younger siblings? Your parents will soon be too old to care for them. Your father is a sick a man. He may not last for much longer. Your siblings look up to you.

You have already taught them how to read and how to understand basic algebra and geometry. Don't you owe them the opportunity to complete their education? Don't you think they deserve your help growing up? Instead, you would be deserting them, leaving them to the tender mercies of life. If you started their education, you should finish it; they are attached to and even dependent on you. They have nobody else. If you desert them, they may grow up as orphans. Accepting this order to be drafted would be a most irresponsible course of action in light of these moral duties to your family. You always talk of wanting to find out what is good and then conduct your life toward that good. If you desert your family and your friends now, you will be undermining your own philosophy.

"We have to move, now! I must admit that we have been too passive for too long. We have known for a while that it would be only a question of time until you are drafted. We have just been sitting here waiting for I do not know what. It should never have gone this far. We should have helped you leave the country before you received the draft notice, when it would have been easier to get you out. We just did nothing. We could and should have convinced you to leave and helped you logistically and morally. Our passivity over the last few months is frankly ridiculous and shameful. It is time to take matters into our own hands and move on. You must pack up your things now and come with me. I will make a few phone calls and make all the arrangements. You will leave this house in the next few hours. We will move you to a safe house where the authorities will never find you. Then, in a few days, we'll get you safely across the border, and that will be it. You will not be able to return to this country in the near future. But maybe in a few years, the stupidity of this war will dawn on everybody, and then nobody will care that you broke the law by leaving the country to avoid the draft. You may then be able to return. Even if you are unable to return, exile in a pleasant, welcoming country where you could continue to philosophize is far superior to death in a stupid war.

"Time is very short now. We must act immediately, or it will be too late. Socrates, as your friend, as your fellow resister to this war, and as your philosophical student, I appeal to you, I beg you, let's go now! I will never forgive myself if you go to this stupid war and get killed. If you die, I will lose my best friend. I know that if I lose you, I shall never have another friend like you.

"Many people know that you are my best friend and that we both object to the war. If you go to this war and become a victim of the immoral incompetence of this government, they will accuse me of sparing money and efforts to save you, or say that I did not care enough for you. I would suffer the greatest shame if people believed that I valued money over the life of my best friend. Nobody will believe that you did not want to escape to save your life and refused my offers of help, though I have been asking you for weeks to let me arrange your escape out of the country."

Socrates shrugged. "Come on, Chris, since when do we care about public opinions? Indeed, why should we? We only care what good people think of us, and they will inquire about what actually happened before forming judgments about our actions today."

Chris disagreed. "We live in a democracy. The opinions of the majority of the citizens matter. We are at war now because most people think they support it. We hope there will come a day when most people realize it was a mistake. If most people come to the wrong opinion about an issue or a person, they can inflict much harm. In a democracy, we cannot ignore public opinion."

"I disagree with you, Chris," said Socrates. "I do not think that the majority of people can do real harm or real good. To harm somebody seriously, they have to make that person foolish. To really do good, they have to make somebody wise. How many majorities do you know that have made anybody more or less wise than they were originally? In the few cases when somebody becomes more or less wise following interactions with the majority of people, it happens by chance, unintentionally. Usually, we become wise by talking with a smart person, and they are always in the minority in any population. If you are a philosopher, a lover of wisdom, you care mostly for wisdom. Since popular majorities and public opinion cannot make you wise, they just don't matter very much."

Socrates stood up and put on a white dressing gown. He walked to the kitchen and made us all Greek coffee. We sat around the kitchen table on that chilly day. We were all ready to assist Chris in his plan to smuggle Socrates out of the country, away from war and into freedom. It would have been easy. We would have helped Socrates pack his belongings—a few items of clothing and a couple suitcases of books—while Chris called his friends to put Socrates on an underground railroad out of the country. In a couple of hours, a car would have come for Socrates, and the next time we saw him would have been in Toronto or some other similarly neutral city. Still, though Socrates was ordered to report to duty within three days and had only a few hours to preempt it, he did not seem to share our sense of urgency.

He sat there in the kitchen calmly and contemplatively and told us, "My dear friends, I want you to know just how much I appreciate your desire to help me, your courage, dedication, and enthusiasm. You feel strongly that you want to do what you believe is the right thing to do and help me. But such strong feelings, such desires, can mislead, take us in the wrong direction. We all agree that we should do the right thing. But first we need to discover what the right thing is, dispassionately, calmly, and without excessive haste. Otherwise, your strong emotions may lead you astray if you do not think the matter through. The stronger the emotions are, the graver could be our mistakes. We do not want to be like the politicians who support this war by manipulating the emotions of their supporters: appealing to their patriotism, their love of fellow citizens and country, and their hatred and fear of tyranny. These strong emotions lead many people to believe they are doing the right thing, whereas as we know this is not true. We must also be careful not to adopt moral stances by imitation, by doing what our friends think is the right thing to do; even friends can lead us astray. We must be careful not to change our views about justice and correct behavior because our immediate interests are adversely affected by doing the right thing. We should not rationalize our passions to make them appear moral, nor should we invent excuses for changing our moral convictions just because suddenly our moral principles require us to make personal sacrifices. We do not want to be like the people who argue that the bus is half empty when they stand outside at the bus stop and then claim that the bus is full the moment they get on. A good method for preventing such biasing of our moral principles by our desires and interests is to keep them stable, to not change our ideas and principles of justice and right action as our personal circumstances change. We cannot allow the natural tendency of people to reformulate what they want in terms of what they hold to be just and right.

"I intend to keep holding to and obeying the same moral principles that I have always defended before I received this draft notice. I have developed my moral ideas on the basis of reasoned arguments. These arguments and the conclusions I have drawn from them have not changed. I am still bound by my commitment to follow them. If I am to revise the conclusions I drew from these principles, we must bring new arguments to this breakfast table. Fear is an emotion, not an argument. Fear of death and hardship can only sway the opinions of children or cowards. To convince me, you need to bring arguments against accepting the legal draft notice I have just received and against enlisting in the military. We agree that this war is unnecessary, useless, and bound to fail, but is that a reason to break the law?"

THE IMMORAL MAJORITY AND PUBLIC OPINION

Socrates continued. "Let us be reasonable and not emotional. How can we rationally decide whether I should obey the draft notice? Let us consider critically your arguments. Your first argument was that I should not join the military out of concern for the opinions of other people who may accuse you, my friends, of failing to help me to escape death or injury or severe hardship, though you are able to help me escape without putting yourself in any serious danger or having to spend prohibitive sums of money on getting me out of this country."

"That's right," affirmed Chris.

Socrates went on. "As you know well, I have always argued that people should not consider what other people think of them but should be selective, caring for what some people think of them while dismissing the opinions of others. It would surely be unreasonable of me to hold this opinion up to an hour ago, before I received the letter ordering me to report for the draft, and then suddenly for no other reason to change my mind and start caring for public opinion. Do I have any reason, other than cowardly fear of death, to drop my selective interest in the opinions of other people?

"I believe that people who expressed opinions on this matter have always held similar views to my own. We should give serious due consideration to the opinions of some people on some matters and ignore the rest.

"Do you disagree, Chris? You have no reason to be afraid. Your back and spine problems released you from military service. You will never be drafted. Your reasoned opinion is not likely to be tainted by fear for yourself, only by fear for me. So tell me, do you disagree that we should consider only the opinions of some people on some topics, and not the opinions of everybody about everything?"

Chris nodded in reluctant agreement. He clearly felt this was no time for entering a philosophical, contemplative discussion; it was a time for action, to get Socrates out of the country. Still, there was no way of moving Socrates without convincing him first.

Socrates was satisfied and continued entirely unhurried. "So, you would surely agree with me that we should consider sound reasonable opinions and disregard opinions that were arrived at through unsound methods or that are unreasoned." Again, Chris nodded his approval. "Good. You will also agree with me then that wise people are likely to offer wise opinions, while foolish people will volunteer their foolish views?"

"Sure, Socrates," Chris confirmed.

"Fine, let us imagine now that we are training for something like a sports competition or for entrance exams to a university, or that we are under medical supervision to improve our health or are on a special diet. Would we care equally for the praise or reprimands we would receive about our progress in training or our pursuit of a healthier way of life from anybody, or would we care only for the professional opinions of the experts in charge of our training: the coach, the teacher, the medical doctor, or the diet expert?"

"I care only for the opinion of the coach," interjected Mitch, who played football in high school and college.

"We should care, be mindful of, and even be hurt when a qualified person criticizes us. We should also be proud of ourselves and be encouraged when the same person praises us. We should not give a damn about praise and criticism from other people. Many people have opinions about how other people should live or train or study, but they have no idea what they are talking about. We should follow the advice and adhere to the rules of conduct that our trainers, teachers, and doctors set for us."

"Yes," we all agreed.

Though he seemed to hammer in the same point repeatedly, Socrates just continued. "Now, what would happen to the athlete who follows the ideas of his fans about how he should prepare for a match but disregards the advice and orders of the coach and the doctor? Surely something bad will happen. Now let us consider what kind of bad effect such a bad decision will have on the person who takes that advice. Let us be precise: which part of the person would be hurt the most as a result?"

"The body will be gone, man," answered Mitch, the athlete, without hesitation. "If you do not listen to the coach, you are going to lose your fitness by underexercising, or you'll exercise too much and your muscles will ache from overstretching and you won't be able to play the game."

"Very good," Socrates cheered Mitch.

The rest of us were not so excited. We were losing interest in discussing sports, coaches, and expert opinions on the eve of Socrates's possible draft in the military, when he needed to escape there and then. Socrates could see that we were getting impatient. He assured us then, "Do not worry. I will not go through any more examples. But you can see what the examples illustrate, the general principle I am driving at: should we be guided by, and care for, the opinion of the majority, or should we follow the advice of the expert, assuming there is one? And if we do not obey the guidance of the expert and instead follow the opinion of the ignorant but vocal majority, we would be hurting ourselves, ruining the part of us that should be trained by the expert.

"If this is true of simple examples, such as athletic training, or preparing for an exam, or following a diet for a medical purpose, it is also true for the important moral issues that concern us today. We consider whether we should follow the experts or the vocal majority in matters of justice and injustice, honor and dishonor, good and evil. If we act unjustly, we would harm not only others but also ourselves, the part of us that should be trained to be just."

As Socrates was finally getting to his point, we became more interested. I was wondering who the expert on justice could be. Who has a comparable undisputed expertise to that of the sports coach or the medical doctor on all matters just and unjust? We encouraged Socrates to continue, as he did. "We can conclude then that when we follow the opinion of the ignorant majority rather than the expert few, the result is the destruction of the part of us that is trained. If athletes train according to the opinions of the fans, they would destroy their bodies."

"Oh, yes," affirmed Mitch, flexing his muscles. "Bad nutrition, too little or too much exercise would ruin your body; you'll look like Ronald MacDonald."

"That's right," said Socrates. "Now tell me, is life worth living with a body that cannot run and jump and dance?"

"Not at all," stated Mitch. "I would not want to live without a good body; I would have nothing to do."

"But what about the part of us that is devoted to justice, the part that recognizes justice and tells us what is just and unjust, the same part that instructs us how to act justly and avoid injustice? If we follow the advice of the immoral majority, we will ruin this just part of us. Is life worth living if the part that gives us the capacity to recognize and exercise justice is destroyed by habitually acting immorally? We would become like psychopaths, criminals, and the henchmen of dictators who, by continuously harming other people unjustly, lose a major part of their humanity, the part that is just and is capable of distinguishing what is just from what is unjust. They are like people who lose their eyesight and cannot distinguish shapes and colors anymore. Could you imagine losing your sense of justice? Would you disagree with me when I argue that the part of us that enables us to sense and distinguish justice from injustice and instructs us how to act justly is more important than the physical parts of our bodies that allow us to run and jump and taste and smell?"

"Certainly." We all agreed with Socrates, as we all cared for justice dearly. Surely it is more basically human to do justice than to taste or smell or run like animals.

"If we agree so far, dear friends, we should worry not about what people in general say about us but about how 'justice' itself judges us, how the experts on justice and injustice will judge our actions today." Addressing Chris, Socrates repeated his earlier point, "Therefore, Chris, your contention that we must consider popular opinion about justice and injustice, honor and dishonor, and good and bad, is ill-founded."

"Yet," interjected Chris, "we do live in a democracy where popular opinion matters. To take the obvious but pressing example, a democratically elected government decided to start this damned war in the first place, and another democratic government is continuing to pursue this war. At least for now, a small majority of public opinion supports the war. If you join the military and then die or become injured in this war, it will happen because of the opinion of the majority, and their misguided ideas of justice."

Socrates shook his head. "What do the two issues have to do with each other? Nothing! I just want you to agree with me on one important issue: it is important that we live well and not just live in the sense of continued biological existence."

Chris nodded. "Yes, we agree on that."

"Then we must agree that life worth living, good life, meaningful life must be just and honorable."

"Yes, we agree."

"On the basis of this agreement, we can examine together whether or not it is just for me to escape this country to avoid military service. If it is just, I commit myself to join and participate in your effort to help me leave the country. If it is unjust, we must cease and desist from trying, and I should obey the order to be drafted. Nothing else matters. The issues concerning your expenses and reputation as a good friend, and the possible prospective difficulties in the upbringing of my siblings, have nothing to do with justice. They are the subjects of fictional stories about betrayal of friends and abuse of children that bad newspapers publish to stir the vulgar emotions of the public. Such strong emotions, uncontrolled by critical reason and rational reflection, are unstable; they change very quickly and unpredictably. If you try to appeal to such vulgar emotions, you will necessarily lose, because they will shift unpredictably, and you will be left, like some aging pop stars, out of contemporary favor. It is useless to attempt to fit our principles of justice to the whims of the masses.

"Inevitably, there is only one issue, and it is the one we must concentrate on from now on: do we act justly if we spend money and put forth efforts to rescue me from conscription and arrange my escape from this country, or would it be unjust of us to do so? If we agree that it is unjust of me to escape, the unfortunate possible outcome that I might die as a result, be injured, or otherwise suffer simply does not matter. The only thing that matters is whether we act justly or unjustly."

Chris agreed immediately. Finally, it seemed like there might be a glimmer of hope that we would be able to convince Socrates to allow us to help him save his life. If we understood why Socrates was reluctant to escape, perhaps we could convince him to be reasonable and allow us to help him leave the country.

Socrates and Chris agreed on the conditions of the debate. If Chris proved that justice demanded that Socrates escape, Socrates would leave immediately. If Socrates proved that it was unjust, Chris would stop demanding that Socrates escape and leave the subject alone. Socrates admitted that a part of him wished he would lose the debate so he could escape, yet he had to obey his moral duty.

JUSTICE AS KNOWLEDGE

Socrates opened this new stage of the discussion by asking Chris whether he thought that people should always act justly and do the right thing, or whether they should sometimes do the just thing and on other occasions act unjustly, depending on circumstances and context. He raised a related question: did Chris think that when people act unjustly, they do so knowingly, or are they ignorant of the injustice of their actions? Socrates said, "If injustice is always the result of ethical ignorance, the problem is not in the bad will—the desire to do evil—of unjust people but in people's ignorance of principles or ideas that help us identify the just course of action. People then must always act justly, except when they do not know what is the right thing to do.

"If by contrast, whether or not we should act justly depends on context, sometimes we should not act justly. People then can act unjustly both willingly and knowingly. For example, suppose a soldier kills a civilian during wartime. If sometimes we should act justly and sometimes we should not act justly, it is unjust to kill civilians in some contexts when they are compatriots, but it is then acceptable (though still unjust) to kill civilians in other contexts when they are foreigners at war with us. If we must always act justly in all contexts, if soldiers kill civilians in war, it is because they are ignorant and confused, because after all that training to kill foreigners who look and speak differently, they cannot distinguish civilians from combatants. If they only knew clearly that it is wrong to kill any civilian in any context, they would have behaved differently.

"If we ought to always do what we think we know is just, justice is always good and honorable. When we commit an injustice, it is then the result of ignorance, of not knowing what the just course of action is. If, on the other hand, we should not act justly under some circumstances, then justice can sometimes be dishonorable and even evil.

"Which of the two explanations of injustice should we choose, Chris? Can injustice be appropriate under some circumstances, or is the same justice appropriate always and everywhere and does injustice result merely from lack of knowledge of the just course of action? Is unjust action sometimes the correct course of action, or does injustice always result from ignorance of justice and not from anybody's conscious will to commit an injustice? When a soldier kills a civilian, is it because the soldier chooses to commit an injustice that is appropriate for that situation, or is it because the soldier is confused or ignorant of the just course of action, avoiding participation in a war crime?

"If our past conduct is any guide to which answer we have already committed ourselves to, there can be no doubt: we have been active in many different civic initiatives, most notably against this war. We have always supported just causes and resisted unjust ones irrespective of context. If we suddenly accept that under some circumstances justice and doing justice are unacceptable or dishonorable, our past convictions and actions make no sense at all. We are not going to start prevaricating like whimsical little children, are we? We should affirm what we have always affirmed, that being unjust is bad and dishonorable always and everywhere. Acting unjustly, in this sense, hurts the person who commits the injustice because it destroys a part of that person that is capable of justice, just as athletes who fail to follow the proper training regime are destroying their bodies as well as harming their teams. Committing an injustice, then, can never be right. Do you agree?"

Chris agreed emphatically. Unlike Socrates, though, he thought that Socrates's impending draft into the military was exactly the kind of injustice that hurts its perpetrator.

Socrates continued. "If we agree that when we commit an injustice, we hurt ourselves as well as our victims, revenge— inflicting an injury for an injury, an eye for an eye and a tooth for a tooth—makes no sense because the avengers hurt themselves, destroy a vital part of themselves, as well as inflict an unjust injury on somebody who was unjust to them. When somebody commits an injustice against us, they harm themselves at the very least by injuring the part of them that has the capacity for justice. We say then that criminals have twisted minds; they are psychopathic, they become less than human by being unjust. If I am right, then revenge and retribution increase injustice in the world rather than do justice. Do you agree?"

All those present in the kitchen found Socrates's argument against revenge convincing and noble. He showed that revenge harms the avenger as well as the receiver of harm. In cycles of vengeful conflicts in places like Northern Ireland, the Middle East, and the former Yugoslavia, both sides clearly lose—not just because both sides kill each other and destroy each other's security and property but also, and perhaps even more so, because they destroy themselves. They become worse human beings. Their obsession with cruel retribution destroys their humanity as well as their ability to empathize with other people and to distinguish justice from injustice. It also destroys their capacity to do justice to strangers and even to members of their own tribe and family. They inflict on themselves a type of disability, just as if they cut off one of their own limbs or blinded themselves. They cannot perceive justice or do justice—as a blind person cannot see and a lame person cannot run.

Socrates appeared somewhat disappointed by our facile agreement. "Do you realize that this contradicts what most people believe? Many people misidentify justice with retribution and even revenge. It is not just difficult to convince such people that they are wrong; it is almost impossible to even talk with them. They just do not get what we are talking about when we discuss justice.

"Are you sure that you agree with me that committing injustice, like harming other people through retribution, harms the person who commits the injustice and that therefore it is better to be the victim of injustice than to be its perpetrator?

Fighting evil with evil, terror with terror, injury with injury is always wrong. Do you agree? Are you sure?"

We were all sure.

"But it seems to me that what you say is an argument against war rather than for conscription," said Chris.

Socrates still seemed to be concerned about whether we truly agreed with his basic principle. "The argument that I want to develop next is based on this assumption. I argue that it is better to suffer injustice than to perpetrate it. Are you certain that you agree with me, or do you wish to express any doubts? If you do, this is the time."

As Socrates knew, our own objection to the war was based on the same principle, that it is better to suffer injustice than to perpetrate it. We were all committed to this position. Had we rejected it, there would have been no basis for our objection to the war and to our insistence that Socrates should choose exile over participation in the war. Socrates, however, sought to derive the opposite conclusion from our shared assumption.

He concluded, "So we all agree that we must always do the right and just thing. Very good! Now, let's see where this assumption gets us.

"We need to apply the principle we agreed on to the current ethical dilemma that I am facing. If I escape this country to avoid conscription, will I do wrong? Will I act unjustly? If I would, then I cannot violate the principle that we agree on. If I do not, then I am free to leave the country to avoid conscription."

Chris replied that he could not imagine who would get hurt from Socrates's escape. He could not imagine anybody suffering injustice as a result. Socrates, on the other hand, could get severely and even fatally hurt if he took part in the war, and that would be a pretty serious injustice.

JUSTICE, THE RULE OF LAW, AND DEMOCRACY

"Suppose I escaped, or ran away, or deserted; different people will describe the same act by different terms," suggested Socrates. "What would be the effect of my action on the Constitution and the rule of law?

"I would undermine the foundation of our democratic society, which is still governed by laws and not by the whims of tyrants, militia chiefs, or petty officials. The rule of law cannot survive if each citizen decides for himself or herself which laws they like to obey and which they do not. If I do not obey some laws because I do not like them or because they are against what I conceive as my interest, other people must have the same right to disobey laws they do not like. My own behavior would then set an example, encouraging others to also disobey the law.

"If each citizen is allowed to select which laws they choose to obey, there will not be any set of rules that apply equally to everybody. Without a universal constitution and laws, society and the state will disintegrate. For example, if everyone refused to pay taxes, the state would cease to function. There would either be no state and no society and everyone would have to look out for themselves, or society would be ruled by the powerful through threats and intimidation, instead of through common laws applied and protected by independent judges. Don't you think that the current situation is better, even if it requires me to go to fight in an unjust war?

"Democracy decides the basic rules of social interaction by majority vote; this becomes the Constitution. On the basis of the Constitution, the representatives of the majority decide on laws. The judiciary is in charge of interpreting the Constitution and the laws. In this way, we can all live together and enjoy the great advantages of social cooperation and civilization without civil wars and violent strife. The alternative could be the war of all against all without rules, or a Robinson Crusoe–style solitary life without cooperation or exchange with other people. Once we live in, or enter, a society ruled by laws, we can expect others to obey the same rules, and that allows us to cooperate, exchange, and benefit from social life in general. If I suddenly exempt myself from the laws that govern conscription, I undermine the rule of law itself and all the wonderful things it enables, the numerous benefits we draw from living together in a civilized society that is governed by laws that enjoy democratic legitimacy.

"Looking at you, I know what you are going to say, Chris. Your eyes are shining. You will try to reverse the argument and present the state as the perpetrator of injustice against me, right?"

"Indeed I would. I think your conscription would be an act of unjust aggression on the part of the state against you," affirmed Chris. "It requires you to involuntarily risk your life on threat of incarceration."

Socrates waved his hands in repudiation of Chris's argument. "In a democracy, the Constitution and the laws are not an impersonal abstract system imposed from above but are rather a form of agreement, a social contract between the citizens who agree to pursue their affairs according to this agreement. If I suddenly escape, I renege on the promise I made to keep the agreement I made by breaking the social contract. I do not think I have any justification for breaking this agreement. Until now, the social contract has only benefited me. The legal system legitimized the marriage of my parents and regulated their relationship and obligations toward me. I then benefited from state education. The laws guaranteed my right to free education, to learn mathematics, the sciences, foreign languages, and how to read and write. Most importantly, this education passed on to me our history, literature, and traditions; it passed on to me our culture. The same state that demands of me now to risk my life according to the law also guaranteed my upbringing and education, according to the same set of laws. I still have no objection to the laws that regulate family relations and education. So, by what right can I single out conscription as the one law I will not respect from now on?

"I do grant you that citizens of states that do not keep their end of the bargain, of nondemocratic tyrannies with particularly bad laws, or of states that do not respect their own laws may not be as obligated as I am to obey a social contract that the state violated. In particular, a citizen the state victimized by violating its own laws, such as failing to protect him from an abusive childhood or failing to provide him with good, free education, has no reciprocal obligation to the state that did not fulfill its duties toward him. If the state does not hold up its part of the social contract, the citizen cannot be expected to fulfill his. But I have no such excuse. The laws were good, and their implementation has been appropriate and beneficial to me.

"In a democracy, if I do not like the laws, I have the right to try to change them, as we have been trying to do. We used all the means that democracy allows: we demonstrated; we wrote and signed petitions; we worked for the opposition; we wrote and published pamphlets, articles, and letters to the editor; we ran for elections and voted for candidates who opposed the war. Still, we failed to convince our fellow citizens to vote in a majority that would oppose the war, and we failed to persuade our legislators to change the government and its policy. Now we must obey the existing laws. We may of course continue to try to change the opinions of the voters and to convince the government to change its policy, but in the meantime, we have to obey the laws. The rule of law brought me into the world, provided me with education, and then provided the safe social environment where I could flourish as a member of this culture and society. Now it demands of me to serve in the military. How can I refuse?!

"If a citizen does not like it here, she or he can leave when they reach the age of legal maturity and seek another homeland. They can take their money and settle somewhere else. But if upon reaching maturity and knowing about the laws and government of the state a citizen decides to remain, the citizen implicitly accepts the laws, including those that may not coincide with their interests, like paying taxes or being conscripted to military service.

"To sum up, there are three reasons citizens should obey the laws of a democratic state: First, even if some laws are not good, the rule of law is better than lawlessness. Citizens draw many benefits from the laws, like security during childhood, education, and a predictable and stable society, before they are called to possibly sacrifice their lives for the laws. People cannot choose to obey only the laws that suit them. If they do, they undermine the whole rule of law. Second, our laws enjoy democratic legitimacy. Most of the citizens vote for them or for the representatives who enact them. Citizens have the right to attempt to change the laws democratically. But if they fail, they accept the results of the elections even if they do not like them. Third, an implicit social contract underlies the citizen's participation in society. If I break the law by leaving the country now, after I received the order to be drafted, I will break the social contract that keeps civilized society together—the rule of law.

"As you know, I have spent practically all my life in this country. Everybody knows that I have hardly left this city. I do not like other places, where people speak other languages and have different customs, histories, and manners of thinking and discussion. I belong here. This is my home, as it was my fore-fathers'. Clearly, this country has not displeased me so far. If I leave now, it is clear that my reason is not a sudden dislike of this country, of its laws and culture. It is clearly my personal interest in avoiding conscription.

"If I violate our implicit social contract now, I will be like a person who signs a contract without reading it. Such a person observes the terms of the contract as long as they are favorable to her but then attempts to renege on her obligations when it comes to paying. I would be like people who take out mortgages for homes or loans for cars they cannot afford, or who buy things on deferred payment programs and then refuse to pay, or who marry and have children and then run away because they cannot face the responsibilities that accompany having a family. Such irresponsible, immature, and short-sighted behavior does not become a philosopher. On the contrary, when I chose to stay in our country, I knew what I was doing. Any reasonable person could have foreseen the plausible consequences of staying here. If I run away now, I will feel as ridiculous as if I took a subprime mortgage, without a job or other assets, and then suddenly, facing foreclosure, sought to annul the mortgage agreement and keep the house."

"Think about Canada," whispered Chris.

"OK," agreed Socrates. "Suppose I escape to another country that is well governed and has good laws, a democratic country that enjoys the rule of law, as you recommend. I will arrive in such a country as an enemy, and all patriotic citizens there will hate me because if I undermined the laws and social contract of my own country, what would stop me from repeating the same in a country that is not my own, under whose laws I have never lived nor accepted implicitly or explicitly? The government and the people of other democracies living under the rule of law would fear that I may undermine their own laws and legal systems, as I have done here. They would most fear that I would subversively influence their own citizens to break their social contract and undermine their rule of law. I would become a perpetual exile, haunted, fleeing from one community and country to the next, always chased away, unwanted and despised."

"If not Canada, then maybe North Korea, right, Chris?" chuckled Socrates. "If I cannot be respected and accepted in other democratic societies that enjoy the rule of law, maybe I should flee to dictatorships where there is no rule of law to subvert, no concept of citizenship, no virtuous state, and no objection to somebody who does not respect the rule of law. The rulers of such societies do not receive their legitimacy from popular vote. They cannot be controlled by an independent judiciary according to their observance and enforcement of the rule of law. Their source of authority is brute force and the power to intimidate and terrorize their subjects. They would be happy to grant me asylum there under their protection, with no freedom, under their control. They could use the story of my escape from a democracy for ideological warfare, to demonstrate that the citizens of democracies flee them for tyrannies, and that the paternal rule of a dictator is superior to the rule of law, and that crafty dictators make better policies than democratic majorities. Will such dictators become my new allies and friends? To what end? So that I can continue to live as their pet, entirely dependent on them? I would constantly worry and try to stay in their good graces, under constant threat that I might displease my masters. What would I get in return? The opportunity to continue my physical existence, to eat and drink. This will suddenly become the meaning of my life as I grow old? Remember, we started this discussion assuming that we want to do what is good, to live justly and virtuously. But in a tyranny? Life as a philosopher under a tyranny is too ridiculous to contemplate.

"You mentioned my young siblings. I would not be doing them any favors if I took them with me into exile, depriving them of the kind of education and cultural heritage that I received and cherish. Surely it would be better for them to stay here and be cared for by my friends. If you are my friends, you will care for them if I leave not just this country but also this world—if I die in the war. It does not matter if I become a soldier or an exile. In either case, their future will depend on how true your friendship and loyalty are. If you are real friends, you will care for my siblings when I am away and unable to care for them, whether I am dead or exiled.

"But this is not important. My life and the quality of my siblings' lives are of secondary significance to that of justice. Justice must come first, or everything else is meaningless. It is better to die in innocence, a victim rather than a perpetrator of injustice, a sufferer rather than somebody who inflicts suffering on others. If I die, it will be the result of the evil that men do, not of the Constitution and the laws. But if I go ahead with what you urge me to do, I shall be returning evil for evil. In return for the folly of our politicians who wish to conscript me to serve in the military for a stupid and unnecessary war, I shall be undermining the foundations of the rule of law, democracy, and the social contract that allows any kind of civilized and just social cooperation between individuals. This unjust course of action will most hurt those who are most innocent, myself; you, my friends; and my fellow citizens. I just cannot do it; my conscience will not let me do it."

Addressing Chris, Socrates said, "Do you have anything else to add?"

Clearly exhausted, Chris lifted his hands helplessly and answered, "Nothing, Socrates. I have nothing further to say."

"In that case," concluded Socrates, "please excuse me. I am allowed to bring a duffle bag with my personal belongings. I have to pack my toothpaste, a razor, and about a hundred books."

A few days later, Chris drove Socrates to Fort Bakum early in the morning. We were all there to see him off. He displayed quiet determination and single-mindedness as he walked, not looking back or displaying any hesitation. For a man about to risk his life for a cause he did not believe in, Socrates appeared strangely at peace with himself and the world.

Later, we learned that Socrates came very close to losing his life in that senseless conflict, but in the end he survived. Facing death, Socrates displayed the same calm resolution as when he debated conscription with Chris and when he left home to go to war. The one thing we would never learn was whether Socrates, who had been shot at, shot at the other side, at people who did not participate in our social contract and did not elect our democratic government.

Most of the young people who debated with and listened to Socrates on that day, however, avoided the draft. Some went into exile. Few disobeyed the order to be drafted and willingly accepted incarceration in military jails for their convictions. More were dismissed by the military as crackpots once they began to argue philosophically with draft boards. (The military made the right call in thinking that those people were not likely to become useful soldiers and that they might have turned combat soldiers into philosophers.) Others used clever tricks to bend the rules to their advantage, feigning a variety of medical, physical, and mental problems to be exempted from military service. Still others used family connections and bribes to land a desk job at a military base near their homes, thereby never getting into harms' way.

We all agreed with Socrates on his two most important assumptions: First, it is better to be the victim of injustice than its perpetrator because being unjust is self-destructive for the perpetrator. Second, since injustice most hurts the person who perpetrates it, the existence of injustice is the result of some kind of ignorance. Justice is always a matter of knowledge; if we only knew what justice was, we would all act justly. But most people do not possess this knowledge or have only a weak grip on it. Majority opinion is no guide for justice. But it is also unclear who the experts are who possess this most important type of knowledge and who can instruct everybody else.

Socrates argued that a kind of social contract obliges us to obey the laws, even when we disagree with them or think they are unjust. This must be an implicit contract, since we never explicitly sign a contract with the state, as we do when we rent an apartment or buy a car. An implicit social contract that nobody actually signs needs to be justified somehow; why should we honor a contract we never considered, agreed to, or symbolized our consent to by signing? Socrates proposed three such justifications. First, the laws are legitimate because they are the result of the democratic process. We are welcome to attempt to affect the results of the process, but we must accept the laws even if they are unsatisfactory. Second, based on the argument from reciprocity, because we have received so much from the state according to its laws—secure childhood and education and so on—we should keep our end of the bargain and obey the laws even when they do not benefit us. Finally, Socrates argued that by not emigrating we implicitly accept the laws of the state or country in which we were born. Had we disliked those laws, we should have emigrated before being faced with conscription.

Socrates's argument about the legitimacy of democratic

laws appeared to some of us to contradict his assumption that majority opinions should not guide us in matters of justice. Philosophers other than Socrates proposed that rights, human and civil, can defend justice from the possible injustices of democratic majorities. Such rights trump the powers of legislatures and voters. The most basic right to life may trump the decision of the majority to require conscripts to risk their lives in the pursuit of an unjust war.

The social-contract argument is difficult to apply to the choices of young conscripts. Conscription usually begins at age eighteen, when people are too young, too inexperienced, too uneducated, too poor, and too weak to run away. To the extent that we can talk about an implicit social contract, its terms are quite unfair. Giving an eighteen-year-old the "option" of leaving the country where he was born is a bogus choice because most eighteen-year-olds lack the material and other resources to be able to leave their homeland and successfully apply to emigrate elsewhere.

Socrates's decision to not go into exile was also affected by his personal love for his homeland. He could not imagine living anywhere else. That was a personal choice that had nothing to do with philosophy, justice, or injustice. Maybe this was the real reason for his decision. His identity and way of life were too intertwined with his country for him to consider surviving in exile. He would have perished in another country, uprooted and alone, and his life would have lost its meaning. There are others, however, in a similar situation who would feel at home in another country, as part of a different culture, and among strangers. Unlike Socrates, the idea of sacrificing their life for the privilege of living in the country where they were born was too much. It was not worth it. Life had to come first.

2

THE ESSENCE OF COOL

(After the *Meno*)

Many people considered Miles to be the coolest guy around. He looked right. He smelled right. He had the right kind of friends. His family had achieved success effortlessly; Miles had relatives on Wall Street, with the federal government, among the higher echelons of the Pentagon, and in the diplomatic service. His parents were rich, politically connected lawyers, and they did not shy away from showering Miles with their wealth. He attended Skidroll College in northern New England, distinguished for being the most expensive college in the United States. Miles had an undeclared major, but he attended several classes in philosophy. He thought they would be easy to pass, and his parents advised him that good grades in philosophy would help him get into a good law school. But he found philosophy to be interesting. He was particularly impressed with the charismatic Professor Georgic, who was reputed to be one of the highest-paid philosophy professors anywhere. Though Georgie never mentioned Socrates in class, at least not in any positive way, his reputation as a thinker and debater had reached Miles. So, when spring break arrived and Daddy loaned Miles his limousine and chauffeur, Miles gathered together some of his best friends from Skidroll College and stopped in New York City to visit Socrates on the way to Florida.

Although he had little in common with Miles, Socrates looked forward to the visit. His mother had been a maternity ward nurse, so his family didn't have much money. He could not afford to attend an expensive college before he was drafted to the military and had never held an academic position. But he liked handsome and charming young men like Miles. So when Miles and his friends caught up with Socrates in Washington Square one afternoon, after having woken up from a night on the town during which they visited some of the best nightclubs and bars in Manhattan, he was happy to converse with them.

Miles and his gang arrived in his chauffeured limo, which he parked right on the square. He knew that if a police officer showed up, he would be able to talk his way out of parking the huge car in a no-park zone. Miles was dressed in a fashionable tailor-made summer suit, and he smelled of an expensive Spanish cologne. Socrates was dressed in a torn T-shirt and jeans. The two men had no problem recognizing each other, even though it was their first face-to-face meeting. Miles examined Socrates, from his unkempt hair and beard down to his old sandals, and smiled to himself as he mentally digested Socrates's shambolic appearance. Socrates appreciatively felt the fabric of Miles's suit, but the proximity to Miles's eau de toilette made him sneeze loudly. When they had concluded sizing each other up, Miles, the more outgoing and confident of the two, addressed Socrates. "As a great philosopher, Mr. Socrates, you should be able to help me with a problem that has bothered me for a while: How do people become cool? Do cool people learn how to become cool theoretically, or do they acquire their coolness through practice, through imitation of cool people, or in an internship with cool people? Or,

if they don't learn it theoretically or through an apprentice-
ship, are cool people born that way and thus are cool by nature,
without any learning or effort? Or do people become cool in
some other way?"

Socrates seemed genuinely impressed. "There was a time,
I still remember, when the students of Skidroll College had a
reputation for being wealthy and for their involvement with
the horse races you have up there. But if your questions represent the level of discussions you conduct these days, you are
going to become famous also for your wisdom. This must be
the result of the college's brilliant and strategic acquisition of
Professor Georgie. His students must have fallen in love with
his wisdom. He must have taught you how to ask and answer
any grand question boldly and directly. We in New York City are
far less lucky, my dear Miles. Georgie must have taken all our
wisdom with him to Skidroll, for the colleges here have fallen
on hard financial times and cannot afford such a prestigious
educator. If you ask anybody in New York whether they think
that people are cool or not by nature or by nurture, they will
laugh in your face and send you back to New England. They
will tell you that they have no idea how people become cool. I
am in an even worse position because I have to admit that I do
not know what coolness or the state of being cool means in the
first place. Until I know what cool means, I cannot answer your
question about whether it is taught theoretically or through
practice, or whether it is an innate quality of people who are
born with it, like the ability to walk and talk."

THE ESSENCE OF COOL

"I am devoid of any knowledge of coolness. Just look at me . . ." Socrates pointed at his torn clothes and protruding belly. "If I do not know the essence of a thing, how can I know its properties? For example, if I did not know you, Miles, I could not know if you were tall or short, rich or poor, blond or dark-haired, and so on. So I am afraid I cannot help you to answer your question."

Miles laughed. He was unsure if he should be disappointed because Socrates could not answer his question, or if he should be skeptical because Socrates ridiculed it. So he replied in such a way as to address both possibilities. "Really? You, the great and famous philosopher Socrates, claim that you do not know the meaning of cool? When I return to Skidroll, I will tell every-body that I visited New York, where I met the great Socrates, and he could not tell me how people become cool because he does not know what cool means."

Socrates did not seem to mind the teasing. "Son, you can tell them back at Skidroll that I have never met another person who, in my opinion, knew what it means to be cool either."

Miles immediately retorted, "You must have never met Georgie. He must know. He knows well such things. He is the smartest person I have ever met."

"Actually, I did meet him," corrected Socrates. "But I do not seem to remember his answer to the question of the cool. Either my memory is failing me or his answer was not that memorable. But this is not a problem. We are lucky to have you here. No doubt, you know Georgie's answer to the problem of coolness and can represent him here. You can either remind us of his answer, or, if you have an answer of your own, then even better, present it here and we will examine it. Considering your admiration for Georgie, I would guess that you prefer to present his opinion as yours?"

Miles agreed enthusiastically.

"Very good," said Socrates. "Since Georgie is not here, tell me what you think coolness means. For goodness' sake, be generous with me and do not be stingy with the wisdom you received from Georgie. Nobody will be happier than me to discover that I was wrong when I asserted that I have never met anyone who knew the essence of cool and that, in fact, Georgie and you know all too well what it means to be cool."

"No problem, Socrates! I will give you a full answer. A cool politician knows how to get elected, how to maintain popularity, how to rule and manage the state. Cool politicians use their positions to give jobs and contracts to friends and allies and to exclude enemies from positions of power and replace them with friends. Of course, it is cool not to harm oneself politically in the process by making powerful new enemies. Sometimes, the cool thing to do with a powerful enemy is to promote them to a position where they cannot do any damage and would not have any interest in making mischief. As the saying goes, keep your friends close and your enemies closer. That's cool.

"Not only politicians are cool. A cool wife and mother stays at home, takes care of the house and the kids and obeys her husband, who works for her and the family so she can do the shopping.

"You see, every type of a person has their own coolness. There are cool young people and cool old people, cool boys and cool girls, cool workers and cool managers, and each one is cool in a different way. When we talk about being cool, we need to recognize that it means different things in different social contexts. There are millions of types of coolness. Not just one. And, note this, Socrates, the same can be said about not being cool. There are many different ways of being a nerd, for example. What is nerdish for one person is not nerdish for another. Professor Georgie teaches that it is important to understand that there are different cools and that each person can be cool in a different way, relative to where they are in society and in life. In the past, colonial European male notions of coolness were dominant, and so people who were not cool in this sense felt like nerds. Following Georgie's work, we realized just how relative the evaluation of how cool somebody is to culture and power. If we study Georgie's philosophy, we realize that there are many different notions of coolness and that we should not privilege our own culture's idea of cool over that of other cultures. He would have said it much better, but this is my summary of his philosophy."

Socrates appeared impressed. "Your ideas enrich me beyond any expectation, dear Miles. I asked for one meaning of being cool, and you showered me with numerous different meanings. Still, you did not answer my question. Suppose I asked you what is a shampoo, and you answered that there are many different kinds of shampoos. There are shampoos for dry hair and for oily hair and for normal hair, and then there are shampoos for dandruff. Some shampoos have a conditioner, whereas others do not. Some shampoos contain extracts from vegetables and fruits like cucumbers and avocadoes; others do not. Some shampoos are for women, and others are for men, children, and babies. Different shampoos have different scents. Georgie and you would tell me that there is no one kind of shampoo that is best for all. Different shampoos are better suited for different kinds of hair. I agree. However, it does not answer the question "What is shampoo?" To answer this question, we need to find a property or properties that all shampoos of all kinds share, irrespective of the many legitimate differences between them. Now do you understand my question?"

Miles nodded hesitatingly, "Yes, I think I do. You would look for something like 'liquid soap'?"

"Yes, but liquid soap is used also in other products, like dishwashing liquids, so it is too broad as the essence of shampoo. I look for what is common to all and only the kinds of coolness that you enumerated. I want to know what makes anybody cool anywhere and anytime, and nothing else. That should be the nature or essence of cool."

Miles still seemed puzzled. "I think I am beginning to understand what you are asking me. But Professor Georgie has never raised, let alone discussed, such questions in class. I guess you would look for something like liquid soap for hair?"

"Let me repeat the question." Socrates reiterated the problem they were trying to resolve: "You claimed that there are different kinds of cool. What is cool for a child is different from what is cool for an adult. Justin Bieber is cool, and President Obama is cool, too. But had either person started to behave like the other, they would have lost their coolness: Bieber's fans would not like to listen to speeches about the economy, and Obama would have lost some of his prestige if he started to sing and dance onstage. The same can be said of health. What is healthy for a small child is not healthy for an adult, and vice versa. Children do not run for long distances or lift weights, activities that are generally healthy for adults, and adults do not eat baby formula, which is healthy for babies. So is there something general that we can call health that both healthy adults and healthy babies share?"

"Yes," affirmed Miles, "health is health whether it is of an adult or a child."

"Right. Then tell me, please, what is coolness in general, whether of a man or a woman, an adult or a child?"

"I can't help thinking that this is somehow different. Being cool is not like being healthy," pondered Miles.

"But why?" insisted Socrates. "You said that a cool politician knows how to manage the state, whereas a cool housewife knows how to manage her household. What is common to these two types of coolness is each person's ability to put their affairs in proper order. Both must know how to act justly and with prudence, and both must have the ability to control their passions to avoid self-destructive decisions out of fear, anger, and so on."

Miles nodded in acknowledgment. "If you seek a general definition of cool, I would say then that being cool is the ability to make people do what the cool person wishes them to do."

Socrates smiled in approval. "Thank you. Finally, you delivered the kind of general definition that we are looking for. But is it a good definition? It seems like it is at once too narrow and too broad. It leaves out clear cases of cool people who do not govern anybody. It brings in clear cases of people who know how to manipulate other people but are not cool. Cool children and comedians do not govern or even attempt to govern anybody. Powerful people who govern unjustly, dictators, and tyrants are definitely not cool. Would you not agree that at the very least you need to add the word *justly* to your definition?"

Miles seemed relieved to agree with Socrates. "Yes, we should add *justly* to govern because justice is cool."

"Be careful, Miles," cautioned Socrates. "Do you want to say that justice is cool, or that justice is a kind of cool?"

"I do not understand the distinction, Socrates," admitted a bewildered Miles.

"I mean, are all cool people also just, or is justice one kind of being cool, and there are also other kinds of cool that are not necessarily just? All just people are also cool, but can some cool people not be just?"

"I think there are other kinds of cool, in addition to justice," opined Miles.

"What are they? Can you give me a few examples?"

"Well," thought Miles, "courage is cool. Prudence and wisdom and generosity are all cool. I am sure there are many other such cool character traits."

Socrates sighed. "Yes, Miles. But again, we return to the problem we had before. We look for the general meaning of cool. But you again propose many different kinds of cool characteristics. We are not exactly back at the beginning, when you said there are many different kinds of cool people in different cultures, ages, genders, and so on. Now you propose different character traits as examples of coolness. This is a bit more concrete and substantial than before, so we have made measured progress. But this still does not lead to the general definition we have been looking for, a common property that all the cool character traits you proposed share."

Miles lifted his hands in exasperation. "I still cannot follow you, Socrates, since I do not fully understand what you want. What is this common denominator of all the kinds of coolness that I mentioned?"

Socrates assumed his pedagogical position. His eyes were piercing, and his hands moved rapidly, like a windmill. "Take it easy, Miles, this is not so difficult. Suppose somebody asks you, "What are cold drinks?" And suppose you answered "Mineral water." Then that person would ask you whether mineral water is the only kind of cold drink, or whether mineral water is *a* cold drink. You would answer that it is a cold drink, since there are other cold drinks like juices and sodas and so on. Likewise, if somebody asked you about the state of being frozen, and you answered "Ice cream," they would ask you whether being frozen means being ice cream, or whether ice cream is a kind of frozen thing. You would then explain that there are other frozen things like ice, fish, and methane gas on other planets.

By saying that sodas and beers are cold drinks and that ice cream and methane on Saturn are frozen, you would not mean that sodas are beers or that methane is ice cream."

"OK, that is obvious," conceded Miles readily.

"So what are cold drinks or frozen things in general? If somebody asks you such a question, you would surely not be astonished. You would not consider the question to be unclear or too difficult but would instead consider what is common to soda, mineral water, beer, ice tea, and so on; and what is common to ice, turkey, margaritas, and methane on Saturn. The definitions should include all the cold drinks or all the frozen things in the world and nothing else.

"Let me ask you the kind of question that probably nobody has asked you at Skidroll College: can you define for me what are cold drinks? Surely you know what they are, as you have been drinking cold drinks all your life. Trying to abstractly define classes of things like cold drinks, or furniture, or animals, or anything else is a valuable exercise that prepares aspiring philosophers to tackle more challenging abstract concepts like justice, beauty, or truth. So why don't you give it a try? Define cold drinks first, and then advance to defining the essence of the cool itself!"

Suspicious of Socrates's hidden intentions or simply insecure about his abilities to define abstract classes, Miles declined and asked Socrates to instruct him instead on how to define cold drinks.

"What will you give me if I successfully define cold drinks for you?" inquired Socrates.

"Anything you want," promised Miles in return.

"What I want most is for you to define what is cool," retorted Socrates.

"Then you shall have it," said Miles.

"For such a prize, I will try really hard," assured Socrates. "How about the following: cold drinks are made mostly of water, are produced for human consumption, and are served at a temperature that is above freezing but below room temperature."

"There is a problem with this definition," a jubilant Miles interjected. "You define one abstract concept, cold drinks, by means of another, frozen. What if the person who hears your definition does not know what frozen is? For example, maybe they live in a tropical country where it never freezes and they have never seen ice."

"Good question," encouraged Socrates. "You follow the Scottish philosopher David Hume, who asked a similar question. I can claim that my definition holds until and unless somebody either disproves it by offering a counterexample or until they offer a better definition. For example, had I claimed that all cold drinks are sweet, somebody could point out that mineral waters are not sweet. But until you offer such a counterexample, or until you suggest a better definition, my suggestion is still the best available. As you may have heard, this is my usual method of inquiry when I do philosophy. I ask people what they think various basic moral terms like *justice*, *statesmanship*, *piety*, and so on mean. They offer definitions, and I bombard them with counterexamples. They then try to offer better definitions that withstand my objections, and then I have to offer new counterexamples and so on. In the meantime, each definition tends to improve on its predecessor because it can withstand the criticism targeted at it."

"Still, suppose I do not know what is frozen," reiterated Miles.

"You naughty boy! You cannot remember Professor Georgie's definition of cool, but you want me to tell you my definition of frozen." Socrates kind of giggled.

"When you tell me what is frozen, I promise to tell you Georgie's view of the cool."

"You are full of promises, golden boy. Your cool charm overwhelms me. No wonder so many people love you. The mere sound of your voice can command people to do as you wish, even if they do not know that you are handsome. But they can infer how pretty you are from the commanding tone of your voice. Only pretty things, while they are still pretty, can be so demanding, yet so charming and cool, as they order people around. You must know that I have a weakness for pretty things, and so you know you can make such demands of me. I must then satisfy your demands and give you an answer, so you like me."

Miles smiled and inquired, "Socrates, are you flirting with me?"

"If I only could, you would have been flattered rather than threatened," replied Socrates. "Though you did not offer a counterexample to my definition of cold drinks, I accept your request not to use terms that may be unclear to the people who hear them. So, I define frozen as the solid state of liquids, as ice is to water. Even people who never saw ice know the difference between solid and liquid and witnessed one turn into the other, for example when fat melts into oil and then congeals into solid again. Is this dictionary-like definition satisfactory?"

"Yes, it is," accepted Miles. "If you could only teach me many more such essences and definitions, I would be happy to stay here with you and learn more."

"For both our sakes, I shall do my best," promised Socrates. "But I doubt I can come up with many more such good answers. I am much better at questioning the meanings others assign to abstract moral concepts like justice and virtue.

"Now it is your turn. I gave you my definition. Now, as you promised, give me yours. You promised to tell me the meaning of being cool. And please remember that you have to propose a single meaning that fits all types of cool things. Do not break it into a multiplicity of little cool things as before, or they will melt and disappear. Do not dissect the concept, or you will kill it. Try to imitate what I did in defining cold drinks and the concept of frozen."

Miles grew silent and contemplative. He then declared, "I think that being cool means to have honorable goals and the power to achieve them. For example, it is cool to say "Yes, we can," because it indicates that the people who say it have the power to realize their honorable purposes and plans."

Socrates wasted no time on praising Miles for finally coming up with the kind of general definition that he was training him to develop. He immediately plunged into a critical discussion of Miles's idea of coolness. He began by asking Miles about the relationship between his idea of the cool and a more general moral concept, the good. "If a cool person wishes to achieve honorable goals, are they also good goals?"

"Certainly," replied Miles. "What is honorable is also good."

"Do you think that some people desire the good, whereas others desire what is evil, or do all people desire what is good?"

Miles replied that he thought some people had evil desires.

"Do people desire evil things knowing they are bad, or do they think bad things are good? Is their problem that they are evil and they know they want bad things, or are they stupid or confused or ignorant?"

"I think that there are both kinds of people. Some people cannot distinguish good from evil and desire what they think are good things, though in fact they are evil. Other people know that what they want is evil but nevertheless want it," replied Miles.

"Are you sure that some people know the difference between good and evil yet want evil?"

Miles confirmed his position.

"Let me just make sure that we mean the same thing when we say *want* or *desire*. We use these verbs in the sense of wanting to possess or to have something. For example, if I want a book or if I desire a particular dish, I want to have them, to possess them, right?"

Miles made a fatal move for his position by accepting Socrates's suggestion that desire always involves possession. He could have argued that evil people do not want to possess evil things but that instead they want other people to possess the evil they give them. Once Miles accepted Socrates's possession sense of desire, it was easy for Socrates to prove that nobody wanted to possess evil things because they would bring harm to themselves. Socrates proceeded to inquire whether the people who knowingly wish to possess evil things believe they will do them good or know they will do them harm.

"As I said before, Socrates, some people think that possessing evil things will do them good, whereas others know they will do them harm."

"Do you think the people who believe that possessing evil things will do them good know they are evil or are they just ignorant or confused?"

Miles denied that vehemently. He held that the people who desired evil did so knowingly and with a clear mind.

"Can we at least agree that people who do not know what is evil because they do not know how to distinguish it from what is good or are confused about it in fact do not desire what is evil; they desire the evil that they think is good—for example, smokers who do not know how bad cigarettes are for them. The people who desire evil things because they think they are good really desire the good. For example, there was a time when people falsely believed that smoking tobacco was good for their health, so high school students were forced to smoke pipes during a plague."

Miles conceded the point readily.

"Now, what about those who you suggest desire evil? If they know that evils hurt the people who possess them, do they know that they will be hurt by them, or do they believe that they will be spared somehow?"

"That is absurd. If they know that possessing evil things hurts the people who possess them, they must know that they will hurt them," said Miles.

"So they must foresee being hurt by possessing evil things."

Miles granted that they would have to lack any foresight not to see that.

"But who wants to be hurt, miserable, and unhappy?!" Socrates rested his case. "If no one wants to be miserable, then no one wants to possess evil, because the possession of evil, the result of the desire for evil, is nothing but misery itself."

Miles felt compelled by Socrates's chain of reasoning to admit that, indeed, contrary to what he had suggested earlier, nobody has genuinely evil wishes because nobody really wants to possess evil and harm themselves. If people wish evil things, it must be because they are confused and unable to distinguish good from evil or because they do not know what is good and evil. Socrates then drew the inevitable implication from this conclusion.

"If nobody desires evil, all humans aim for the good. The fact that cool people also aim for what is good does not distinguish them from nerds or anybody else."

Miles accepted Socrates's conclusion but pointed out that his proposal for defining the essence of the cool was narrower than just the desire to possess good things, which cool people share with everybody else. Cool people, he emphasized again, are distinguished by their ability, their power to possess the good and to benefit from it. "They do not just aspire, because they can also acquire the good. Coolness would then be a power, an ability to attain the good." Miles was comfortable with associating coolness with a kind of power, the power to attain good. After all, nerds are usually powerless.

Socrates told Miles that this time, he probably agreed with him. "Being cool is having the power to attain good things. But what are the goods that cool people want and can attain? Do you think the goods cool people can possess are things like health and wealth, nice big cars like your limo, lots of bling, attending prestigious colleges, getting well-paid jobs on Wall Street, or powerful political appointments?"

"Exactly, Socrates. You got it! I have to admit that you do not look like you'd know the answer, but you do know what good things are after all. Looks may be deceiving. Personally, you may say that I was born to be cool because everybody in my family is cool. My dad works on Wall Street and also attended Skidroll College. My mom is a congresswoman, and before long we hope she will become a senator. Everybody in my family lives in big houses in good neighborhoods, and we all drive luxury cars. As for bling, well, not so much perhaps," he laughed, pointing to a modest gold chain from a famous jeweler around his neck.

Socrates continued to play along: "May we add that the pursuit of bling must be conducted justly for it to be cool, or that it does not matter how one gets the bling, as long as one has the power to possess bling to be cool?"

Miles disapproved of Wall Street crooks, so he replied as his dad would. "Certainly not, Socrates. Cheating, embezzling, insider trading, and Ponzi scheming may get you bling, but they are not cool."

"Then the acquisition of good by itself is not cool. To be cool, this acquisition must be just, moral, or honest. We are looking, then, for some part of ethics, the theory of right action to limit the cool possession of goods to honest mergers and acquisitions and to exclude dishonest ones?"

"Exactly," agreed Miles.

"If we agree that acquiring bling in a dishonest, immoral fashion is definitely not cool, then not acquiring bling in a dishonest fashion must be cool. For example, if somebody refuses to participate in some dishonest financial scheme, like lying to customers about financial products like mortgages or mutual funds or raiding pension plans, that is cool. Nevertheless, the honestly cool banker may miss out on acquiring the bling."

"Honesty is cool, and dishonesty is not cool at all," echoed Miles.

"But then we reached an absurd, self-contradictory result," bemoaned Socrates, "because we agreed that acquiring bling is sometimes cool and sometimes not cool. So acquiring things cannot be important to being cool. The acquisition of bling is both too broad and too narrow for being cool. It is too broad because some acquisitions, dishonest or fraudulent ones, are not cool. It is too narrow because refusing to acquire wealth by dishonest means is cool. Earlier, we agreed that the pursuit of good things is universal, so it cannot distinguish cool people from nerds who desire the same things. Instead, we reached the conclusion that justice and honesty are cool, and what is dishonest and unjust is uncool."

Miles accepted the inevitable conclusion. "This is certain."

"But surely you are making fun of me. It is not nice to mock an older man like this! You make promises, and then you break them."

Astonished, Miles protested, "But how?"

"We had an agreement and you broke it! We agreed that you would deliver to me a nice whole, undivided, unabridged, complete meaning of coolness. Earlier when I asked you what is cool, you told me about parts or kinds of cool things, but never the whole concept. Then I gave you the example of defining cool drinks for you to imitate. I thought we agreed on everything, and instead, you deliver coolness to me all shattered and broken into little pieces, as before.

"You must have forgotten everything we talked about and agreed on because you reached the conclusion that cool is attaining good things justly. Therefore, justice is a part of being cool. So, according to you, being cool is about things that cool people do with a part of their coolness, namely, justice. So, again, instead of proposing what is the meaning of cool, whole and undivided, you just told me about a part of it, justice. You defined cool by a part of it, by doing things justly. But you cannot define the whole by its part. It is like defining a car by having a steering wheel, or a house by having a door. If I already know the whole, I can learn something by learning about its parts, but not the other way round. If I know what a car is, knowing that it must have a steering wheel helps. If I know what a house is, it also helps to know that it has a door. But a door does not help me know what a house is, and a steering wheel does not tell us what a car is. In the same way, accepting that cool behavior is just does not tell us what is cool. So I am forced to return to the point where we started and ask you again: what is the essence and meaning of being cool?

"In our search for being cool, we cannot rely on justice. As you remember, following your own demand, we agreed that we cannot define one concept by means of another equally unclear concept. You made me define frozen when I used this concept to explain the meaning of cold drinks. So, if we need to use justice to explain the meaning of cool, we have to explain the meaning of justice, which I guess would be at least as difficult.

"But let us be diligent and not give up. Can you tell me what you, or that great mentor of yours, Professor Georgie, thinks being cool means?"

Miles lifted his eyes to the sky in total exasperation. He was clearly losing his patience with Socrates, nervously twitching, brushing off invisible specks of dust from his jacket, and jingling his car keys. "Socrates, Socrates, you certainly live up to your reputation. I have heard about you before we met today, of course, and you exceeded my expectations. I heard when people discuss philosophical problems with you, they leave the discussion even more puzzled than at the beginning. You hypnotize, cast an argumentative spell over your interlocutors. You lead them along a line of argument that looks promising, make them agree with each of your premises, and the deductions and inferences you draw from them, until they reach a result that is self-contradictory or otherwise absurd. Then we have to go back and wonder, where did we go wrong? We must have gone wrong somewhere to reach such an implausible conclusion. We must have been wrong to accept some of the premises you introduced, or we were wrong to follow some of your inferences from them—who knows? At this stage, at the absurd end of the discussion, I am too tired to inquire. We end up being more confused at the end than at the beginning because you manage to shoot down any positive proposal I made, but at the end, the conclusion you reach is even more ridiculous than any of the unsuccessful conceptual balloons your interlocutors float, which you so diligently explode with your argumentative pin.

"How do you manage to get away with this? You know what you are? You are like a torpedo fish or a stingray. You hide, and then when you see your prey, you numb them, not with an electric current like the fish but with the shock of your fluent argumentative force. You also look a bit like a torpedo fish, with your round figure and thin legs. Right now, my mind has been torpified, I am numb and weak and can hardly move. I cannot answer you anymore. My tongue sticks to my teeth.

"I have heard many people talk about being cool, including Professor Georgie, but this does not help me now to answer your question about the essence of the cool. You are quite dangerous in your ability to confuse people about the basic concepts they hold that form the basis for their way of life. I think you are wise to live in this megacity with all its human diversity and tolerance of different, eccentric, and strange people with even stranger ideas. If you went to live somewhere else, a more stable community with traditional systems of belief might regard you as a subversive. You could end up in jail."

Socrates gave his version of a giggle. "Miles, sweetie, you tease me. I know why you compared me to a torpedo fish, fat and round, but with an electrifying sting."

An innocent-looking Miles denied having compared Socrates to a torpedo fish in that sense. Socrates replied that he thought Miles wanted Socrates to call him names, too. Pretty boys like it when they are compared to animals. Yet Socrates refused to "oblige" Miles by calling him names. "I may be only partly like a torpedo fish. I may indeed give a kind of intellectual electric shock to my students, but I also shock myself. As much as you may feel confused and bewildered, I am genuinely even more perplexed. I do not know what the meaning of cool is any more than you do. The only difference between us is that before you met me today, you thought you knew what it meant. I used my electric shock—or, from another perspective, magic wand—to awaken you, Sleeping Beauty, from your dogmatic slumber rather than to numb you. But let us join forces and inquire again together: what is cool?"

KNOWLEDGE AS MEMORY

The long philosophical discussion with Socrates had its intended effect on Miles. It trained his mind to vigorously think philosophically. Like a well-trained athlete, he could use the same set of skills acquired through practice to play different games. So far, Miles and Socrates were playing a value and meaning game; they were discussing character traits like coolness, justice, and the good. They attempted to clarify the meanings of these concepts and in the process had to consider the method for clarifying difficult abstract concepts. Though they eventually failed to find out what is being cool, Socrates concluded that, like all forms of good character, being cool must be just.

Now Miles raised a new sequence of questions in the theory of knowledge, or epistemology, to use the professional philosophical term. He asked Socrates, "How can we inquire further into the meaning of cool if we do not know what it is? Generally, how can we ask questions about things we do not know? If we do not know them, what are we asking questions about? Even if we do stumble on the correct answer, how would we know it is correct? For example, we asked questions about the meaning of cool. Suppose we found the correct answer. How would we know it, if we do not know in advance the meaning of cool?"

Socrates turned sympathetic. "I know what you mean. It seems like it is impossible to conduct any inquiry about anything. We either inquire about things we know or about things we do not know. If we inquire about things we know, there is no point to the inquiry because we are not going to learn anything new that we do not know already. If we inquire about things we do not know, we do not know what we are inquiring about, and so the inquiry is impossible. Right?"

"Perfect. You agree with my argument then?"

"Actually I do not."

Miles seemed to have decided to reverse roles with Socrates and become the questioner. Imitating Socrates's posture and tone, he inquired, "Why don't you agree with me? The argument seems sound enough."

"Because of my grandmother," replied Socrates.

"Your grandma?" asked an astonished Miles.

"Yes, my grandmother," affirmed Socrates. "Also my great aunt; they were very close. They dabbled in the occult together. They held séances, read mystical stories; I think they also smoked mushrooms together to expand their consciousness. It was the sixties, you know."

"These are your sources of wisdom?" inquired Miles in disbelief.

Socrates shrugged off Miles's astonishment "Well, one must find ideas where they are available. My grandmother babysat me quite a lot when I was a boy. I heard many of her stories more than once. She believed that every human being has a soul. She also believed that that soul is eternal and immortal. Life can end, but in death the soul leaves the body and is later reborn in another body, but it is never destroyed. Death is not the end but a new beginning. The legend tells that after death, the soul has to spend time atoning for all the bad things it did in life before it can be reborn. According to the Pythagorean myth that my grandmother followed, this has a lot to do with eating beans."

"Beans?" wondered Miles.

"Well, you know, beans can have demeaning effects. Pythagoreans advise you then to avoid eating them, like Muslims and Jews advise you to avoid pork. If you gorge yourself with beans in this life, you have to work it out of your soul in a kind of vacuum in the afterlife. When you are done, then your soul is pure and ready to be reborn. The less beans you eat, the quicker you will be reborn and the holier you will be in your next life. If you avoid beans altogether, you would be perfectly holy, and you may be reborn as the queen of England or somebody else equally free of beans and their effects."

"I'll bear that in mind next time I dine at a Mexican restaurant," promised Miles.

"That would be prudent of you," agreed Socrates. "Be that as it may regarding beans, if the soul is immortal and has been reborn again and again in an endless cycle of birth, growth, death, and birth again, the soul may acquire knowledge both from its existence in various historical periods and social contexts, and from what it experiences on the other side when it deflates itself from the effects of beans. What the soul needs to do, then, is 'remember,' as it were, what it already knows from all its past experiences. An inquiry, a search for knowledge, then, is an attempt to remember what we already know. Learning is a kind of recollection of what we already know. It is like when you know that you know something like somebody's name or the code for the ATM or where you left your keys, but this memory is just not immediately available. You use all kinds of tricks to help yourself remember, like associate the missing memory with something that you do remember, like when you give your ATM code the same date as a historical event. Teaching, the art of pedagogy, is not transferring knowledge from a knower to somebody who does not know but is instead is a kind of reminding, triggering a memory of knowledge that is already there. Since all souls have such recollections, anybody, irrespective of intelligence or background, is capable of learning, as long as they are ready to concentrate and focus on attempting to find out answers that are already in them.

"This is a very optimistic conclusion for philosophy: anybody can be a philosopher if they are ready to try hard enough to recollect what is in them already. Philosophical inquiry is possible because we are not ignorant about what we inquire, nor is it redundant because we already know whatever we wish to inquire about. We need to pursue our inquiries actively to achieve recollection. This active pursuit of recollection is the method I have been using in my philosophical inquiries. I never teach anything to anybody because I have nothing to teach. I only try to help them recollect what they know already by asking them questions about it. Would you like to start again our inquiry into what is cool?"

"Yes, but first I would like you to teach me just one thing: what exactly do you mean when you claim that we do not learn anything because what we refer to as learning in everyday language is actually just a process of recollection?"

Socrates started again to giggle. "Miles, you are such a tease. You ask me to teach you, just after I argued that there is no such thing, only assistance in recollection of what the student knows already. You are trying to trick me into contradicting my own theory in my practice. Naughty, naughty, you clever boy, but you will not succeed. I have nothing to teach you or anybody else."

Miles appeared to be taken aback by Socrates's severe accusation. "But, no, Socrates, I was not trying to trick you to contradict yourself. I was just using a manner of speech that I was used to. After all, most people talk about teaching and learning and not about recollecting. If you are right, the phrase 'to teach' is like the phrase 'to break someone's heart'—a linguistic remnant of the ancient belief that the heart rather than the brain is the seat of emotions. But I do wish you offered a more convincing proof of your theory of knowledge recollection. You mentioned your grandmother and great aunt as the source or at least inspiration for an occult theory about the rebirth of souls that do not eat too many beans. This does not seem designed to inspire much confidence."

"No, it does not," acknowledged Socrates. "If you prefer scientific mumbo jumbo to the occult, I can tell you about genetically transferred instructions for the hardwiring of the brain as selected by biological evolution. The structure of the brain determines how we conceptualize the world. These conceptualizations tend to reflect how the world, or at least a part of it, really is because they endowed our ancestors with evolutionary advantages, which were then passed on to us. This explains our concepts of banana—food, and snake—danger. It was helpful for the survival of our ancestors up there on the trees millions of years ago to recognize foods and dangers. However, this does not do much to explain our concepts of car batteries, the Greek gods, and quantum particles. Most of the concepts we know today would have been useless just a few hundred years ago, let alone during the millions of years our ancestors were mouselike creatures hiding from dinosaurs and venturing out only at night. Most significantly, nobody knows anything about the mechanism by which information is stored in our genes and then transferred from one generation to the next.

"Still, whatever that mechanism is by which we possess knowledge without knowing it, it can be elicited through questions that assist anybody to recollect what they already know. Let me give you an example or, better still, a demonstration. Tell me, what is the most difficult class you take in college?"

"That would have to be logic," replied Miles. "So many students failed it that the administration decided to stop listing it as a required course for philosophy majors. As an elective, only few students register for it. It is just a very difficult class to teach, even for teachers who know this stuff very well, and it is a very difficult class to study for, even for students who otherwise do well in philosophy classes."

"Maybe the problem is not with logic but with the attempt to teach and study it, rather than recollect what is already known. Let me show you what I mean. That chauffeur of yours, who has been waiting so patiently in the car while we have been talking here; does he speak English?"

"Sure, he has been working for my father since forever."

"Excellent. May I borrow him from you then for a few minutes? I promise to return him whole and unbroken."

Miles waved to his chauffeur to come and join them. He introduced him to Socrates and explained to him that Socrates would ask him a few questions and that he should try his best to answer them correctly. The chauffeur agreed. Socrates asked the chauffeur whether he had ever attended a class in logic or read any logic textbooks. The chauffeur laughed. He had never been to college, and in his spare time he read the sports and funny pages in the newspaper.

"Excellent!" exclaimed Socrates. "You are exactly the sort of person I am looking for. Let me ask you a few questions or riddles. I will tell you some assumptions, maybe they are true, maybe they are not. It does not matter. I just want you to tell me what follows from them, OK? Ready, let's start. Suppose that all human beings are mortal. And suppose that I am a human being. What then?"

"Then you are going to die," concluded the chauffeur.

"Bravo!" exclaimed Socrates. "Now suppose that all the Greek gods are immortal, and suppose that I am a Greek god, even if I do not look like one."

"Then you will live forever."

"Bravo again. Now suppose that all humans are mortal and

all gods are immortal. And suppose that I am either a god or a human. Then what?"

"Then you will either die or live forever."

"Very good again. Now, suppose that if anybody is a god, they must live forever, and suppose that I drop dead here and now?"

"Then you could not possibly have been a god."

"Wonderful again. Now, suppose that if anybody is Greek, they must speak the Greek language. Suppose I speak fluent Greek. Then what?"

"Umm," said the chauffeur. "You could be Greek. But then you could also be an American who studied the Greek language and became fluent in it without being Greek."

"And right you are again," cheered Socrates. "But are you certain that you have never received any instruction in logic or at least read a logic textbook in your spare time? Because you have just used syllogism, modus ponens, and modus tollens."

The chauffeur burst out laughing. "Modus what? I do not know any modus. Ask me about four-wheel drive, and I'll explain something I know about."

"Oh, no, you know quite a lot about logic. You just do not know that you know. But let me be sure about what you have just said. Have I just taught you logic? Have you learned anything from me?"

The chauffeur shrugged his shoulders. "I don't think you taught me anything or that I learned anything. You just told me some if this/then that–type statements without asserting anything as true or not."

"We call them conditionals," interjected Miles.

"And then you asked me what was the conclusion, and I told you what came into my head. I know no logic. I would need to go to college to learn that. They would have to teach me the answers to the kind of questions that you put to me. Otherwise, I would not know the correct answers. That is why rich people pay for their kids to go to college. My dad was not rich, so I could not go to college and I did not study logic, so I don't know any. If it is so easy, why do people go to college?"

"I don't know why people pay for their kids to go to college. But I do know that you know logic. In each case, you came up with the right answer, and each answer required the application of a different logical principle. The only thing you did not know was the names logicians gave to each type of argument. Everything else was there before I asked you anything. I did not teach you; I just helped you recollect what you already knew."

Turning to Miles, Socrates added, "You have been to college for a few years. So you must already know that the best teachers you have had and ever will have are those who do not try to teach you anything at all. Teachers who lecture and dictate and post bullet points on websites do not make you wiser or make you know anything. The philosophers who make you wiser are the ones who teach you nothing at all and do not even attempt to convey any knowledge to you; instead they just do their pedagogical work by asking you questions, guiding you on your own intellectual journey to where you can find the answers you know but cannot recall. Am I right or not? But you know it already."

"Yes, I know it already," acknowledged Miles. "Bad teachers just lecture, and it goes in one ear and out the other, even if we retain something of what they say when it's time for the exam. The good teachers make us think by challenging us and asking questions."

"What about your chauffeur? We—and, indeed, he himself—say that he does not know logic, yet he was able to apply to my questions perfectly logical laws that he had never studied."

Miles agreed.

"And the same is true of people who think they do not know things in general. They do not know that they know. They are in a dreamlike state from which they need to be awakened to realize what they know, just as you may need a moment to recollect who you are, where you are, and what got you here after a deep sleep. If I went on to ask your chauffeur more and more questions from different directions and in different forms, and if he went on being cooperative and didn't get bored or distracted, he would eventually achieve the level of proficiency in logic that an advanced student of logic would have learned at college."

Miles agreed with this conclusion as well.

"In reply to your question about knowledge: obviously knowledge is not acquired, for as we said, your chauffeur has never studied logic. He must have possessed this knowledge before, but where did it come from? The inevitable conclusion is that he, like everybody else, was born with this knowledge, and this knowledge originated from somewhere, even before he was born. Whether that origin was the previous lives of the soul, as my grandmother claimed, or in the genes, as more contemporary thinkers propose does not matter for this conclusion."

"That is an inevitable conclusion," affirmed Miles.

"If we agree on this, then you must accept that knowledge of things like the laws of logic must precede life and persist after life ends. The part of the soul that possesses this knowledge must be immortal. Mind you, I am not talking about the survival of our individual memories and desires, nor am I suggesting that knowledge can take on a physical form such as is portrayed in films, where souls are presented as semitransparent beings. I am talking about the survival of true knowledge that is not individual or special to any person but is rather a universal truth shared by all, like the laws of logic. Truth is eternal, and so is the part of the soul that possesses it."

Miles smiled. "I like what you say. It is nice to know that part of us is always going to be and that we only need to try to remember it to know it."

Socrates smiled back. "I also like what I am saying. But I am less confident of some of my assumptions, especially the part about my grandmother's spiritualism. It would be nice to know of some process that would explain how knowledge of things like the laws of logic is transferred to us prior to birth. I use words like *remembrance* or *recollection* to describe the possible relationship between the innate knowledge we possess without acquiring and the knowledge we become aware of through my method of inquiry: asking questions without presuppositions. Yet, *recollect* or *remember* are metaphors. I do not mean literally remembering memories, like we remember what we had for breakfast. It would have been nice to state this relationship more clearly. Still, it is encouraging to know that all our inquiries have a solution within us. If we only pursue knowledge with sufficient perseverance, we will remember. We can reject the skeptical proposal that there is no knowledge, or that even if there were any, we could not find it unless we already possessed it. The pedagogical implication that education should be based on dialogues, questions and answers, and questions about the answers, rather than on dictations and learning by rote, is particularly appealing."

"Here, too, I find no disagreement between us," reiterated Miles.

BACK TO THE COOL

"Great. So let us go back to your original question," declared an invigorated Socrates. "We agree that we can raise questions about things we do not seem to know because through the process of questioning we may recall them. What does that mean for our search for the nature of being cool?"

Encouraged, Miles agreed enthusiastically. "Let me repeat, if you do not mind, my original question: do people learn how to become cool, are they naturally cool, or do they acquire their coolness by some other way?"

"If I were you," replied Socrates, "I would still start the inquiry with an attempt to understand the nature or essence of the cool before getting into a discussion of whether or not it can be taught, as we did before, unsuccessfully. But you are you. When you drive, you pay no attention to traffic rules. Instead, you make sure that your chauffeur obeys the rules, and then you call it a joyride. I cannot stop you from asking a question about the properties of something we do not know, especially since you expect me to answer that question. Since you appointed me your philosophical chauffeur, you must allow me to attempt to answer your question by using the hypothetical method. This means that I will pose a hypothesis without claiming that it is true, and then see if it can deduce or infer an answer to your question. Scientists often have to pose such hypotheses before they are able to confirm theories. For example, Newton assumed hypothetically that an object in motion continues in motion in a straight line—or, vice versa, an object at rest stays at rest—unless other forces affect it. Together with a couple of other such ideal hypothetical presuppositions, Newton was able to explain all movement in the universe, including that of the planets around the sun. As you probably remember, when I helped your chauffeur realize that he knew logic, I presented him with hypothetical assumptions that I neither proved nor claimed were true. I then invited him to deduce conclusions from those hypothetical assumptions according to the rules of logic he knew but did not know that he knew. If we pose a hypothesis and it explains a wide scope of different kinds of things and problems that interest us, it proves at the very least that it is a useful hypothesis and may even be a true one. If the hypothesis does not do much explanatory work, if it explains only a narrow range of things, and if it is inconsistent with everything else that we know, we may well want to drop it.

"The hypothetical method, applied to our attempt to answer your question, means that we hypothesize what is cool without proving it and then see if this hypothesis explains whether or not coolness can be taught. Then we examine whether this result fits what we see around us in society. If it does, there is a case for arguing that the hypothesis is useful and perhaps true.

"My hypothesis is that coolness is a kind of knowledge. I do not claim that it is true. But I want to examine what follows. I think it is easy to deduce that if it is knowledge, then like all knowledge, it can be taught. But bear in mind that when I use the word *teach*, I mean *remember* or recollect rather than to receive the knowledge from without. I use *teach* and *recollect* here interchangeably because I do not distinguish between them, and in ordinary everyday language, we talk about teaching. We should not debate semantics, the meanings of words.

"If we agree that the hypothesis that being cool is a kind of knowledge implies that it can be taught, what happens if it cannot be taught?"

"Then the hypothesis is false and its opposite must be true. Being cool could not be a kind of knowledge," said Miles, completing Socrates's sentence. "It is like saying that if you are a human being, you must have a brain. If you do not have a brain, then you cannot be a human being. That is a no-brainer."

"The logicians call this form of argument *modus tollens*. But apart from this label, you, like your chauffeur, already knew everything about this logical argument before you came here. You just applied it now to the new hypothesis that I introduced: that being cool is a form of knowledge. We added the conditional: that if it is a form of knowledge, then it must be possible to teach it. Then you made the obvious deduction that if it cannot be taught, being cool cannot be a form of knowledge."

Miles nodded in agreement as Socrates continued, "But this is not the only hypothesis that we should examine. Another possible hypothesis is that being cool is a good, like being healthy or being wise."

"Yes," agreed Miles. "This seems highly plausible given everything we know about being cool. But then what is the relationship between your two hypotheses? Are they different but complementary? Do they contradict each other? Do they compete in some other sense over being the best explanation of our experiences of coolness and cool people? Or are knowledge and what is good connected with each other?"

"Very good questions," encouraged Socrates. "Let us consider the relationship between knowledge and what is good. Being wise is a good and is obviously a form of knowledge. Being healthy is a good and may be connected to the knowledge of how to eat right and how to exercise correctly and so on. So, what is good can be a form of knowledge. If so, then the question of whether being cool is good is reduced to the question of whether being cool is having knowledge.

"Another possibility is that not all goods are knowledge. If this is true, then cool could be a good that is not knowledge. I think anybody can agree that being cool is a type of good, so we do not need to prove it."

"Yes, that is obvious," said Miles.

"Would you also agree that all types of good things benefit us somehow? If so, being cool should benefit us as well, yes?"

Miles agreed. "Yes, I think all good things benefit us. Health is good and it is obviously beneficial. The same is true about wealth, strength, and beauty; they all benefit the people who possess them."

"True," said Socrates. "But those same goods can also harm us. We read all the time about rich, powerful, and beautiful people who came to a bad end through some form of self-destruction. Perhaps if they had been less rich or beautiful or powerful, they might have had a longer and better life. In some cases, wealth, power, or beauty can harm rather than benefit those who hold those qualities."

"Lord Acton said that all power corrupts and absolute power corrupts absolutely. Wealth, beauty, and so on make people more powerful than they otherwise would have been. Thereby, it also makes them more corruptible, more susceptible to self-destruction. Weaker people do not have the means for elaborate forms of self-destruction. If they try hard, they can still manage, but it is more difficult. Think, for example, of Marilyn Monroe or Anna Nicole Smith. Their beauty, a good, did not do them much good."

"If you can call that beauty," said Socrates. "But would you agree with me that when all these goods are used appropriately, they benefit their holders, and that when they are misused, they harm their holders?"

"Yes, sure. Had Anna Nicole Smith used her money to buy a philosophical education, which would have taught her how to live right, as well as the meaning of life and how to reach it, rather than drugs, it would have benefited her. Had dictators like Saddam Hussein used their power to help and support their people rather than to oppress them and start wars, it would have benefited them and others."

"We can distinguish the goods that are forms of knowledge

from those that are not. It is striking to note that all the goods that do not involve knowledge sometimes benefit the person who possesses them and sometimes harm that person. Consider even good character traits that do not involve knowledge, like self-control, courage, intelligence, generosity, and so on. Courage, for example, is a character trait that everybody agrees is good. Yet without caution, risk assessment, and prudent planning, a courageous person can become excessively confident and therefore invite danger, whether he is a soldier who dies running in a minefield or a banker who loses an overly risky investment. The same holds for intelligence and self-control. If they are not guided by wisdom, they can harm their holders. An intelligent person can fall in love with their own clever models and not see how reality can predictably diverge from the models because of minor interventions by factors they cannot consider and because of the effects of unintended consequences. Self-control can be emotionally insensitive, unintelligent in some contexts, in the absence of wisdom that can direct a person to show their emotions when expression of empathy or sympathy is appropriate.

"Can we conclude then that wisdom guides us toward benefit, while stupidity leads in the direction of misery?"

"This is a version of your earlier argument: that being good and virtuous is generally a form of wisdom," recalled Miles. "This is an appropriate argument for somebody who is a philosopher, a lover of wisdom, I guess."

"Yes, but I am still on a hypothetical level here. Bear in mind that I am not claiming that goodness is a type of wisdom; I just presume it, run with it a bit, and see where it gets us, OK?"

"Yes, sure. Run along."

"Quickly, then: If being cool is to be beneficial in all contexts, always, it must be a kind of wisdom and excludes stupidity. Since being cool always benefits cool people, it must be some kind of wisdom. Generally, any character trait can be beneficial or harmful. It all depends on the wise or foolish governance that directs the character. You can think of character as the mechanism of a car and of wisdom at its steering system. The best-engineered car in the world will be useless, or could even wreak havoc, unless a wise driver controls the steering wheel. So what really benefits the person, the source of all benefits, is wisdom. To return to our original question, we must conclude that being cool is either wholly the same as being wise, or that it at least partly includes being wise."

"Well, that is the conclusion I have expected you to reach. Hypothetical method or not, you claimed earlier that people do evil only when they lack the knowledge of what they are doing. So it all fits."

"Almost, almost there," said Socrates. "We conclude that all absolute, context-free goods, including being cool, are forms of wisdom. Wisdom is not attained effortlessly by nature, like the ability to walk and talk. It needs to be learned. This fits nicely with what we can all observe in everyday life. If people were born with their characters as natural endowments—some babies cool, others intelligent, still other brave—it would have been possible to discern so in their childhood and to predict which cool persons would become great actors and politicians, which brave men would make great generals, and who would excel at university. It would have made sense to segregate the exceptionally gifted children and raise them separately, since everybody would have been certain of their future place in society. There are attempts at doing this, especially at discovering intellectually and artistically gifted children, only the intellectually gifted usually come from financially successful families. If it were all about nature, there would be no reason to nurture; educational opportunities and good teachers wouldn't help anybody."

"Indeed, good education is very valuable," agreed Miles. "Since good character is obviously not produced by nature, it must be produced by nurture. Therefore, coolness is knowledge that can be taught."

"It would seem so, but, alas, not quite."

"But why? I thought we agreed on everything at this point. We eliminated the possibility that coolness is a natural gift, so the only other alternative must be that it can be taught. We also discussed several examples. So how could we go wrong?"

"If being cool is knowledge, it should be possible to teach it. Like all other kinds of knowledge, there should have been classes for it, teachers and students, textbooks and exercises. But there are none. Arts for which there are no teachers or students probably cannot be taught."

A still-doubtful Miles inquired whether Socrates could be sure that there are no teachers who instruct people in how to become cool.

"Oh, trust me, Miles. I have been looking far and wide and for years for people to teach me how to be cool. I went to extraordinary efforts to locate them, all in vain. Also, my friends who cared for me wanted me to become cool, and these are people with wide networks of contacts. It seems hopeless.

"But let us not give up. Maybe Ronald Drumb here can help us."

Socrates pointed to the famous Ronald Drumb, who was sitting next to us, amusing himself by listening to Socrates and Miles's conversation. Drumb was very cool indeed. The son of a self-made multimillionaire, he was nevertheless a modest, unpretentious, and low-key man. He gave his children the best education money could buy, in addition to bestowing on them his attention and the lessons he had learned from his long career. Though he grew up in a wealthy family, Ronald joined his father's business and worked hard to expand it, displaying

in the process considerable business savvy. He was also politically active nationally and locally. He had been elected several
times to powerful political offices. In the meantime, he had
many lovers, countless wives, models, and actresses, and financial advisers. Drumb was cool. There was no question about
that. If there was anybody who understood the meaning of
cool and could tell us anything about how to become cool and
remain so, it was Ronald Drumb. If it is possible to teach how
to become cool, Drumb, the best practitioner of the art of the
cool, would be the best tutor in the world.

Socrates turned to Ronald Drumb and asked him if he
could consult with him for a short while on the topic of the
cool, so that he might assist him and Miles in their search for
teachers of coolness. Socrates, as usual, suggested we start first
with asking an easy question. "Suppose your daughter or son
wanted to become a medical doctor. Where would you send
them to study?"

"With the best doctors, of course, Johns Hopkins Hospital
and Medical School, probably," replied Ronald Drumb.

"And if they wanted to make shoes for a living?"

"Then I would send them to learn this craft in Milan, Italy,
with the best shoe designers and manufacturers."

"And so on?"

"Sure, if they wanted to be journalists, I'd get them intern-
ships with the *New York Times*. If they wanted to be engineers,
MIT and then Boeing."

"Let me take just one more moment of your time to ask you
one last question: when we agree that if your child should want
to become a medical doctor we should send her to study with
medical doctors, is it because those doctors are accomplished
practitioners of medicine, or is it because they claim that they
can teach anybody who pays them and is ready to learn? If we

send our children to study with professionals, is it because they are superb practitioners or because they are offering to teach them for appropriate tuition?"

"Of course we choose the best professionals. There are many shady universities that sell degrees to anybody who pays them. Over time, they acquire a bad reputation, and then their graduates can't find jobs or they get fired because they received a poor education. This is particularly prevalent in the kind of state universities where the bureaucrats in charge reward or punish the schools based on how many students graduate. Those schools then graduate anybody, even if they do not bother to come to class. The education market is just like any other market. 'Buyer beware!' is just as relevant when it comes to paying for your education as it is for buying a used car. You have to ask how far will it get you, and you have to look under the hood."

"Can we conclude then, from the cases we have considered, that good education consists of studying with professionals who know how to teach them? For example, if we want to study how to play a musical instrument, we would attend a conservatory or take classes with an excellent musician, yes?"

"Anything else would be really stupid," affirmed Drumb.

"Then can you please advise Miles here? He wants to be cool and go into politics like you, become an upright and notable citizen, a celebrity even. He wants his parents to be proud of him and his achievements. Where and with whom should he study how to become cool? Who claims to teach people how to become cool? Life coaches? Gurus? Self-help authors? Psychotherapists? Image makers? Campaign managers? Spin doctors? Fashionable academics with simple theories that explain everything? If you pay them, they will try to teach you how to be cool."

Drumb's face became red with anger. "Shysters, witch doctors, fraudsters; I'd fire the lot of them. I hope that none of my children, relatives, friends, or fellow alumni will ever approach those types in search of being cool or wise or anything else. They are pests, confidence tricksters, at best a nuisance."

Socrates wiped his brow. "This is truly shocking. Of all the professionals who claim to improve the people who pay them—academics, art teachers, athletic coaches, and so on—it is only the ones who have to do with building character, or at least the public image of a character, who are not only useless; they can actually harm people's characters by corrupting them, by teaching them to be cynical, manipulative, narcissistic, and deceptive.

"This is crazy indeed! However, it is not the shysters who sell these services who are crazy but the fools who pay them for such services, be they adults or the parents who send their children to expensive colleges to study from such charlatans, like Professor Georgie at Skidroll College."

Drumb was still angry. Socrates asked him whether any of these professionals had ever hurt him to make him so angry. But Ronald Drumb denied any personal connection or knowledge of them. He had nothing to do with them, nor would he have anything to do with them.

A polite and sensible person would and perhaps should have left it at that. It was obvious that this was a sensitive and sore issue for Ronald Drumb. But Socrates never let social niceties get in the way of his dogged search for truth. Socrates had no love for the professions Drumb derided. Socrates had been even more critical of them than Drumb had been. Yet he could not help himself. He asked Drumb how he could know anything about these professions—whether they are good or bad—if he is wholly ignorant of them and did not know anybody who works in them?

Drumb dismissed Socrates's question with a wave. He did not need to know people to know what kind of people they were. He was sure of his judgment of them.

Socrates pretended to be impressed. He praised Drumb for having clairvoyant and prophetic powers; otherwise, he said, how could Drumb know so many things about people he had never met? Still, he decided not to pursue this line of inquiry, since the purpose of the discussion had been to discover who could teach Miles how to be really cool, not to identify the false teachers who would not teach him anything good but who would take his money and leave him worse off. Socrates asked Drumb to recommend who could teach Miles to become a cool, eminent, and upright citizen like Drumb himself.

Clearly in a bad mood now, Drumb told Socrates not to bother him and to tell Miles from whom he should study how to become cool. Socrates hastily appeared to be admitting his mistakes and asking for Drumb's help when he said, "I told Miles whom I think his teachers could be. But that was before I heard what you had to say. I learned from you just how wrong I was. I have to admit that everything I told Miles was wrong. You cannot leave us in such a state of ignorance. You have to tell me now where Miles can learn how to be cool, so I can give him a good advice. Please tell us whom you would name as Miles's teacher if you could make the choice."

Still annoyed with Socrates, Drumb retreated to patriotism. "Why do you want me to recommend a particular individual? Any adult American patriot can help Miles. We are the coolest nation. Just take him to meet some decent tax-paying patriotic citizens in places like Virginia or North Carolina or even some parts of Massachusetts. I would not recommend Vermont. They will teach him good old traditional American values, and he will become cool enough!"

Socrates persisted, asking whether the upright, patriotic American citizens who could instruct Miles were born that way and could therefore instruct others in the wisdom they possessed since birth, or had they been instructed by others.

Drumb replied, "They must have been educated by the previous generation of American patriotic citizens. Patriotic traditions are made of many generations. We have had many, many such generations of patriots in this country." He added, somewhat aggressively, "What is your problem, exactly?"

Socrates appeared to be accommodating again. "Indeed, there have been many good patriots and citizens in this country, as well as excellent statesmen. This tradition has not gone extinct; we still have many patriots and great statesmen, engaged and active citizens. There cannot be any doubt of that. But the question that has been bothering us is whether these good patriots and citizens have also been good teachers of their own virtues, virtues like being cool. Have these good people of our own and previous generations been able to teach their good character to others? Or is it true that good character cannot be communicated, taught, or transmitted from one person to another? That is the question that has concerned Miles and me. Consider some of the great statesmen and patriots of American history: Jefferson and Franklin, who founded the United States; Lincoln, who saved the Union; and, more recently, President Ronald Reagan, who won the Cold War. We can all agree that they were great American patriots and statesmen. But consider their children . . .

"If anybody could be a great teacher of patriotic virtue and coolness, it must be such people. Yet only rarely do such people have children who are as cool as they are. Sometimes, it is possible to explain the failures of the children of great patriots by citing parental neglect. Sometimes these people are too busy caring for their nation or for humanity to be actively involved in bringing up their own children. But most children learn many different skills from their parents: how to speak, for example, or how to drive, and yet they fail to learn how to be cool from people who were the coolest of their generation. Parents often want their children to inherit their skills, social status, professions, and so on. Cool parents are likely to do their best to make their children as cool as they are by educating them and purchasing the best education that can be bought. Yet it is rare for such people to have children who match their accomplishments. The children of cool parents are on average no more or less cool than anybody else. How can it be possible to teach someone how to be cool if even very cool people cannot teach it to their own children?!"

Ronald Drumb's anger reached the tipping point where anger turns into menace. Drumb stared straight into Socrates's eyes and threatened him: "Socrates, your criticisms of the great heroes of our nation are entirely unacceptable. You have no right to speak like this. This is unpatriotic. If you want my advice, it is for you to be careful and shut up. You are questioning the beliefs that unite and support our nation. This would lead patriotic citizens to question your patriotism. Are you just of Greek descent or were you actually born there? Or are you an illegal immigrant, maybe? Can you show me your birth certificate? How would you feel about going back to live in Greece? From what I read in the newspapers, the economy there keeps slipping into a recession as if it were sliding down a slope lubricated with olive oil. If I were you, I would have been more careful not to antagonize my adopted country." Drumb threw his plastic coffee cup into the garbage, motioned to his chauffeur, and drove away.

Socrates did not appear to react to Drumb's outburst. He turned to Miles and said, "I seem to have enraged Mr. Drumb.

You know why he is so angry? He did not understand that I was only interested in the question of whether being cool and possessing other good character traits can be taught. He misinterpreted me as attacking the good reputation and memory of the founders of our nation. He considers himself to be one of them, so he takes it all quite personally. If I note that George Washington had no children of his own; that he adopted Martha's four children from her previous marriage and that the only one to reach maturity was spoiled and unpatriotic; or that Benjamin Franklin's only son to reach maturity was on the loyalist British side in the War of Independence, he feels like I am talking about his own children. They are not as shrewd in business as he is, you know.

"I believe that when he stops thinking about his frustrations with his own children and understands what our discussion has been about, he will forgive me. Anyway, it does not matter. I do not work for him, so he cannot fire me. Let us go back to the topic of our dialogue. Do you think that the teachers you have at Skidroll College attempt to teach you how to develop a good character, including how to become cool?"

"Members of faculty disagree on this issue. Some argue that college should contribute to building the character of its students. If that is the case, college teachers must display superior moral character. But other teachers, including Professor Georgie, laugh off this attitude as old-fashioned and unrealistic. They claim that college professors neither possess a superior character nor know how to teach it. College instruction, they claim, is instrumental. If you want to get from point A to point B, good education can tell you the shortest route, the cheapest way of getting there, or the history of getting from A to B. But it cannot tell you whether point B is worth going to or whether we should forge our character so we can make it to point B. Questions of character and value are all about goals rather than instrumental means. Professor Georgie emphasizes that philosophy is not about life and the world but about representations of life and world, about language. He does not think that academic philosophers can or should try to teach how to live or what is good in life or what kind of character people should have. He thinks philosophers should teach only how to analyze texts and how to use language to convince other people. Much of it is about learning how to write and talk persuasively. Well, everybody knows that a degree in philosophy is a good preparation for law school. That is why my dad advised me to choose philosophy as my major."

"Surely the professors who neither claim to know what good character is nor know how to teach it cannot teach you how to be cool. Do you feel that the other educators you had in college who do support the teaching of good character influenced your character—for example, taught you how to be cool?"

Miles laughed. "Those nerds?! Please. Even if they had known how to be cool, they are too deferential to students who pay the kind of tuition fees that my dad pays to criticize us for anything. They just entertain us in class, flatter us, give us good grades so we get into good law schools, and then hit our parents for donations."

Socrates laughed at Miles's admissions and summed up the discussion. From the dialogue with Ronald Drumb it emerged that people of exceptional character who are especially cool cannot teach even their own children how to be cool. Miles's experience at Skidroll College indicates that professional teachers cannot teach their students how to become cool either. Exceptionally cool individuals and professional teachers would have been the most likely people to be able to teach someone how to be cool. Since they do not do so, it may well be that there are simply no teachers of the cool to be found anywhere. If there are no teachers of how to be cool, there are no students either, no scholars, no research fellows, just no one.

Miles agreed. But then he raised a most basic question: "It is obvious that the world is full of cool people. We cannot deny that. They are all around us. So where did they come from? If they did not learn how to be cool from the previous generation of cool citizens, and if they did not take classes in coolness from professional teachers, and if they were not born that way, how did they acquire this highly desired character trait?"

"We must have made a mistake somewhere, then," conceded Socrates. "Reality does not seem to fit our hypotheses. We can either dump reality, claiming that it is an illusion, or concede that there must be something wrong with our hypothesis or the way we derived our conclusions from it. Since I do not want to lose touch with reality, we must save it from our theories. Let us trace back the argument to see where we could have gone wrong.

"We assumed, hypothetically, that being cool is a kind of knowledge. But we did not consider that good and correct action, including cool behavior, can happen without knowledge. People can act cool, even if they do not know what they are doing. If we deny that it is possible to act rightly without knowing what we are doing, we simply cannot explain the world we live in."

Miles seemed confused. He wondered how people could be cool without knowing what they are doing. Socrates suggested it was simple. "A broken clock is correct twice a day. Now, imagine that we are all broken clocks. Some of us are bound to get it right sometimes. We may resemble passersby who give strangers directions. Some people are reluctant to admit that they do not know the correct direction, so they just point at a direction randomly. Sometimes, this random direction can also be the correct direction. From the perspective of the person who received a direction in a strange city and reached their destination, it does not matter whether the guide made a lucky guess or shared their knowledge of the city plan. They got where they wanted to go. Successful guesses can be just as effective in the field of finance. Successful financial managers and investors can make profitable decisions without knowing where the market will go simply by making lucky guesses. In a famous experiment, an economist chose an investment portfolio by throwing darts at the stock listing page of a newspaper. This randomly chosen portfolio outperformed most professionally managed investment funds. If all such investment decisions were made without knowledge and solely on the basis of lucky guesses or opinions, some managers would do better than others, though occasionally they would all do well; we call that an economic boom. If, on other occasions, they all made mistakes, we call that an economic bust. But knowledge would have nothing to do with it. These investment managers never know what they are doing; sometimes they form the right opinion by coincidence, while on other occasions, they form the wrong opinion. If they are extremely lucky, one or two managers may make the correct call repeatedly, but that will happen because among thousands of managers, some will be luckier than others. They will not be able to repeat their performance systematically, nor will they be able to teach their methods or train other people in them, because they have no methods; they do not know themselves how or why they were successful. For this reason, it is impossible to teach business like we teach theoretical fields like physics, nor is it possible to train people to become successful investors as one may train a medical doctor or an air-conditioning technician, because there is no knowledge that can be transferred."

An astounded Miles challenged Socrates: "So what do people go to business school for?"

"For networking purposes mostly, I guess. The mathematics is also true irrespective of its applications. Business law teaches what is illegal and how to perform economic activities like conveyance of property. Otherwise, students just read success stories about lucky people who formed the right opinion without knowing what they were doing. True opinion can be just as pragmatically useful as wisdom based on knowledge.

"We missed this when we falsely assumed earlier that knowledge is necessary for right action and character. This was wrong because correct opinion can also lead to successful actions and character."

"But there is a difference," interrupted Miles. "Wise people who possess knowledge will always get it right, for example, when a great chef cooks the same great dish over and over, or when an accomplished musician plays a piece perfectly again and again. People with right opinions will get it right only some of the time. For example, a taxi driver who really knows this city will always give you correct directions. But a visitor who does not want to admit that he is from New Jersey, and just gives directions at random, will only be right some of the time, and he will mostly be wrong. Similarly, no financial manager or investor always gets it right. Even the most successful ones like Warren Buffett and George Soros make mistakes sometimes."

Socrates congratulated Miles on his analysis. "The only problem left is to explain how people with the right opinion can nevertheless take the wrong action."

The mystery of wrong action following right opinion seemed to confuse Miles; it was too much to handle. So Socrates volunteered to answer his own question. "When you were a child, did your parents ever buy you a balloon filled with gas?"

Miles laughed. "Yes, of course. But why do you care for bal-loons suddenly?"

"Do you remember the basic trick with such balloons? You must keep holding them. As long as you do, you can enjoy them. But the moment you lose your grip and let go, it flies away, and neither you nor anybody else can catch it again and bring it down. True or correct opinions are like balloons filled with gas lighter than air. While we hold them, they are beau-tiful and useful. But by their nature, they tend to run away from us. We rarely can hold on to them for very long, unless they are tied to us somehow. This "tying" in the case of opinions is our "remembering" them, because they are already with us, as we have already discussed and agreed upon earlier. When we rec-ollect, we have knowledge. We tie the balloon to our hand, and no matter what we do and where we go, the balloon remains with us. That is why knowledge is so superior to true opinion or what is sometimes called true belief; it remains tied to us, like a balloon on a string. As you know, I profess my ignorance of most things. I am really sure of only very few things. But if there is one philosophical conclusion I have reached that I am sure of, it is of the distinction between knowledge and true belief. On the level of a single action, true opinion may be just as useful as knowledge. The person who acts on the basis of true beliefs is just as effective and successful as the one who acts out of knowledge."

"And this is your explanation of the meaning of cool?" Miles jumped to the conclusion. "Cool people, though they have no knowledge that they can teach others or transfer to their chil-dren, still possess true beliefs?"

"Neither knowledge nor true belief are natural or nurtured by society. People are not born cool or not cool. Nobody studies how to be cool. There are no schools or teachers of charm or cool. Cool people have been unable to transfer their coolness to their children and students. If it cannot be taught or transferred, coolness cannot be a form of knowledge. The only option left is that cool people possess right opinion that guides their actions. All sorts of successful people possess right opinions, true beliefs. But they have no reason for their opinions. They do not understand how they reach these right opinions. These people include investors and fund managers, politicians, psychotherapists, and so on. Like the prophets of old, they possess something like divine madness, which allows them to say things without understanding them. This is the magic of being cool or making great investments. Since they do not possess knowledge, they cannot teach it to other people. So, it all seems quite magical. Compare them with scientists and applied scientists. Since they possess knowledge of the universe and how it works, when they apply this knowledge, we know exactly why it works and what the limits of that knowledge are, and we can predict reliably that this knowledge will go on working effectively. You never know when and why a financial manager might lose her magic touch and begin to lose money. You can predict that certain medical treatments will always work for certain medical problems because the medical doctors have real knowledge. The same is true for applied physics and chemistry, engineering. This is the difference between science based on knowledge and magic based on true opinion."

Miles agreed with Socrates but wondered what Ronald Drumb would think of it. Would he accept that the founders of the United States had no understanding of what made them take right actions and be cool? George Washington was cool, but did he know why?

Socrates answered that he could not care less what Ronald Drumb thought. His own success as an investor, no doubt, was based on right opinions that Drumb neither understood nor could teach to his children. Socrates summed up his discussion with Miles: "Being cool comes at the bequest of neither nature nor of nurture. It is a kind of innate disposition that some people possess for no apparent reason. This innate disposition is not the result of reasoning and knowledge. Had cool people possessed knowledge, they should have been able to teach it. There seems to be not a single person, however cool, who is able to teach others how to become cool.

"Still, we will never know anything for sure or gain deep understanding of these issues until we understand the truth of what it is to be cool, what is the essence of the cool. I am afraid we did not make much progress on this front here. We eliminated some opinions. We connected the idea of cool with the ability to achieve good things justly. But then, despite our earnest attempts, we failed to connect it with wisdom or knowledge. The good news is that you do not need to understand coolness to be cool, any more than you have to understand economics to be a great investor."

Miles smiled with deep satisfaction. "This is where I should head, investment banking. I am cool already. So, I can be a cool investor, and I do not need to know anything. That is just great. Thank you, Socrates! No wonder everybody praises you so much. You really helped me feel much better. You should come to Skidroll to give a guest lecture." He laughed, hailed his driver, gathered up his friends, and drove off to Florida.

We heard later that the conversation with Socrates changed Miles's life. Despite his father's wishes, he decided to study for an MBA rather than apply to law school. In the fullness of time, his father forgave him. Business can be just as cool as law.

3

GOOD, EVIL, AND GOD

(After the *Euthyphro*)

Why on earth did Socrates want to teach at the religious Agora Preparatory School for Boys in Virginia?! He should have known that it would not end well for him. We were astounded when our friend and mentor packed up his books and went south. Socrates was the sort of guy you would see sitting outside the New York Public Library, or in Washington Square, or sometimes on the boardwalk on Brighton Beach. He was always conversing with friends and acquaintances or entering into conversations with complete strangers. He would start by asking an innocent, mundane question and end up discussing anything from the meaning of life to the essence of the cosmos. Some people enjoyed arguing with him, others sought to avoid him after one heated dialogue during which their most cherished beliefs were undermined, and still others did not know what to make of him. Was he a sage, an eccentric, a madman, or all three? Socrates was born and lived most of his life in the metropolis. His way of life—who he was—seemed intertwined with New York, with the constant interaction with new people and ideas. Why did Socrates seek to forsake it all for a denominational boarding school in rural Virginia?

"The good life," explained Socrates to his bemused friends. "There is no one for me to argue with in New York anymore."

His friends were puzzled. Was he not constantly surrounded by many students and admirers? But Socrates's friends did not understand my old teacher. Socrates craved debating with people who *disagreed* with him. Admirers were of no use to him. They would not debate with him, and so he could learn nothing from them. In New York, his reputation for being undefeated in philosophical debates preceded him, intimidating potential interlocutors. Unchallenged, Socrates became bored.

But, Socrates said, "High-school-age students do not know how to be intimidated. Fresh minds have new ideas. I shall be able to debate again. Hurray!" He chuckled and boarded a Greyhound bus to Richmond.

Socrates enjoyed challenging authorities who used their powers or prestige to impose their opinions on others. He ridiculed people who adopted the opinions of others because of who they were or because they had power rather than considering the quality of their arguments. "Experts and academics can make mistakes like the rest of us, just more so because too few people dare to oppose and correct them. Philosophical debates cannot be resolved by bureaucratic means or according to power hierarchies," he used to say. Socrates, who had no claim to being an expert and little formal higher education, took special pleasure in demonstrating to formally educated experts how little they knew. But his wisdom and reputation made Socrates into a recognized authority on philosophy. Unintentionally and against his will and wishes, Socrates became an expert. Surrounded by friends and admirers, Socrates could not practice his favorite activity—debate. He could not search for the truth by interrogating others, questioning their and his beliefs and unreflective assumptions. He could not live as a philosopher among admirers, and so he had run away to a remote place where he was unknown and—considering he would be teaching at a denominational school—where most people would disagree with him and would likely neither respect nor admire him.

After he left, we heard from Socrates only sporadically. He was happy teaching at the Agora Preparatory School in a small Virginia town and was very content with the debates he had with his students; they always disagreed, and, though it took some effort, he trained them to not be deferential to him.

But it didn't take long before trouble arose. Soon, the news was everywhere. Concerned parents began asking the school's management board to relieve Socrates of his duties for allegedly corrupting their children by casting doubts about religion and asking them to question their patriotism. Socrates was not going to give up without a serious debate. While Socrates prepared to defend himself before the board, I traveled to Virginia to be with him during the hearings. I must admit that I had missed the company of my old mentor and the pleasure of listening to him debate and question and ridicule authority.

I accompanied Socrates to schedule the formal hearing before the management board at a large neoclassic building in downtown Richmond that housed the offices of several religious organizations. In the lobby, we ran into the famous television evangelist, the Reverend Hugh Thrip. Socrates's fame—or notoriety—undoubtedly preceded him, for Thrip's cherubic, plump face smiled at us broadly as he said, "Oh, Socrates, the famous teacher! Playing truant again? That is no example for your students! What brings you here? Are you pursuing or running away from God or men?"

Socrates smiled back. "I have to answer some accusations about my teachings before the Agora Preparatory School for Boys management board, whose offices are in this building. A young father who goes by the name of Mel Etuxor charged me with corrupting his kids. I'll be the first to concede that Mel is to be congratulated for recognizing the importance of education. I also think education is very important. Unfortunately, we seem to disagree about what good education consists of. He claims to know how children become corrupted, what kind of education corrupts then. He even knows who is personally responsible for corrupting his kids at school."

Socrates looked at his shoes in mock shame, as Thrip stared at him reprovingly. Socrates stared back and smiled apologetically. "Mel does not care much for television either, I am afraid. He considers it an instrument of corruption."

Hugh Thrip shrugged and tapped Socrates on his shoulder in solidarity, saying under his breath, "The Lord can use more than one instrument for his purposes, however imperfect the instrument."

Socrates thanked Thrip for his kind reassurance and continued. "I consider Mel to be luckier than me. He thinks he already knows everything he needs to know. So he has nothing more to learn. Unlike Mel, I think I do not know anything, so I try to learn from smarter people who know what I do not. It is just so difficult to find them. Meanwhile, I honestly confess my ignorance about important issues such as good and evil to my students in the hope that they may be able to teach me or refer me to somebody who can. Mel thinks that ignorance or at least the admission of it corrupts the youth, and so he complained about me to the authorities.

"Mel wants his kids to become good citizens, so he cares about education, just as he cares about the corn he plants so it grows and is worth being harvested, cut, dried, fried, flattened, and made into flakes. Mel will first take care of those he considers to be the sources of the corruption of youth. Once he eliminates all the corrupters of youth, he will then proceed to take care of all the other corrupters he sees everywhere else. He will treat society as he treats his cornfield with pesticides. I foresee a great political future for him."

Thrip bit his lip. "It is hard to believe that ignorance is the reason for dismissing a high school teacher. If we go on like this, who will remain to teach?! Tell me, what does he claim you do to corrupt the youth?"

"Mel Etuxor makes the strange claim that I invented a new religion and that I deny old-time religion. He thinks I attempt to convert my students, including his children, to this new religion and cause them to denounce the religion of their forebearers. As he puts it, since this is a religious nation united under God, he must defend America and its faith from me."

I expected Reverend Thrip to sympathize with Socrates's accusers. After all, he was a conservative televangelist with opinions probably not far removed from those of Mel Etuxor. But I was in for a surprise.

"I know exactly what you are going through, Socrates," said the reverend. "The the scandal-seeking journalists also accuse me of inventing a new religion. They say I only pretend to follow traditional religion. They are slandering you just as they have been lying about me. They excite the emotions of the gutter-tabloid readers and TV viewers to increase their circulation and ratings. They do not mind telling lies about anybody just to create a scandal. Whenever I speak of what God told me, or when I heal the sick, or if I perform a miracle or two, the journalists always poke fun at me. They present me as a con man and accuse my followers of being stupid or mad. Yet I heal and perform miracles. There are many testimonials to the success of my miracles. They ridicule us because they envy the blessings that God has bestowed on us. We should not pay them any attention. I say: carry on, Socrates, with your good works and pray that our detractors become enlightened and save their own souls from eternal damnation for ridiculing us!"

"My dear Reverend Thrip, you are indeed experienced in handling public ridicule!" exclaimed Socrates. "However, my problem is a little different. Ordinary people do not mind clever fellows as long as they keep their love of wisdom to themselves. They become angry when a lover of wisdom spreads wisdom by making other people wiser by proving to them that they have not been as wise as they thought. Teachers, parents, management boards, government bureaucrats are all united in attempting to prevent wise people from becoming teachers. Whether it is because of envy, as you put it, or for some other reason, I do not know."

"My dear Socrates, this is not *my* problem. The world can rest assured; I am not a teacher, nor do I want to become one. I shall not train for free more television evangelists. The competition is tough enough as it is."

"Indeed, my dear Thrip, we seem to have different problems. You have no interest in teaching your vocation to others. But my desire to teach and learn keeps getting me into trouble because I teach everything I know, which is nothing!"

"Nothing?" wondered Thrip. "How can you teach nothing? How can anybody get angry at you for teaching nothing?"

"The realization that I know nothing has been my greatest intellectual achievement," protested Socrates. "Most of the mistakes people make result from not realizing how much they do *not* know, the unknown unknowns, as one defense secretary famously put it. I know just how ignorant I am and try to spread this great insight. Realizing how much we do not know requires criticizing what people think they know but do not: common, conventional opinions that people share without reflection; orthodoxies; and dogmas. Outside of the classroom, my lessons are free to anybody who is ready to listen to me because I have nothing to teach but knowledge of what we do not know.

"If the management board of the Agora school wants to poke fun at me, as the media ridicules you, Hugh, it is just fine with me. I should be happy to accommodate them. I admit there is much to laugh at when looking at me. But I fear that their intentions may be more sinister. The ultimate result, whether or not I lose my job, may be divined only by prophets like you."

Hugh Thrip gave Socrates his reassuring million-dollar smile. He was confident Socrates would keep his job, even if it took a miracle. Socrates had at least one advantage: he could argue his own case better than any lawyer—that was another thing the two men had in common; Thrip was also acting as his own advocate. Socrates inquired as to whether he was prosecuting or defending.

"I am prosecuting, Socrates. I am prosecuting my own son before the First Athenian Congregation's council of elders. I want to disown him and expel him from our congregation. I expect this to lead to another media circus. A conflict in the family of a holy man like me is too juicy for the media to ignore. Even members of my own family and congregation begged me to stop. But I know I must pursue this case because it is the right thing to do!

"You may not believe this, but my own son is guilty of disobeying his father! Does it not say in the scriptures 'Fear thy mother and father' and 'Honor thy father and mother'? I sent him to college to study marketing and finance so he can inherit my ministry and acquire an honorable profession. But instead, he switched to philosophy and religious studies. How will he ever be able to take over the ministry from me with such an educational background? To top it all, he has a girlfriend who is a Methodist! And the two of them moved in together. My own son, a sinner, a fornicator! Those who try to make excuses for my son to dissuade me from disowning him do not know right from wrong. I do! We must set an example for others to follow."

Socrates and I were stunned. Disagreements between children and their parents are common. Disowning one's son, turning him into a stranger, is extreme. Since Thrip was on his way to the offices of his congregation to file a formal request to expel his son, I suggested that we have lunch in a nearby diner and discuss the matter more thoroughly, before he did something he might regret later. I hoped Socrates would be able to dissuade him from doing anything irreversible. Perhaps it was not too late to save Thrip's family.

Thrip agreed. He drove us in his SUV in silence. We settled at a quiet corner table where we could talk. Thrip ordered a cheeseburger with fries and a large soda. Socrates and I asked for lamb gyros with lentils and a glass of wine.

GOOD AND EVIL

Socrates opened the discussion by asking Thrip whether he was sufficiently certain of his knowledge of good and evil to unhesitatingly disown his son. Did he not fear that he might make a moral mistake in judgment and consequently harm his own son unjustly? This line of questioning did not get us very far. Thrip was certain of his judgment and affirmed without any hesitation that he knew right from wrong. His son was wrong and deserved to be punished.

Socrates appeared to give up without a fight. He accepted Thrip's judgment deferentially. I had witnessed Socrates's method countless times before. He would assume his famous stance of Socratic ignorance and encourage the person he was talking with to "teach" him. Then things would get complicated.

Socrates said, "Since you are far more certain about your moral judgments than I am, it is appropriate that you become my mentor and teach me how to distinguish right from wrong. I will become your pupil and disciple. Undoubtedly, once I am reborn as one of your followers, it will be easier for me to refute the malicious lies of Mel Etuxor. If he accuses me of being irreligious and an inventor of new religions, I shall tell everybody that I have become your disciple. Some of the members of the management board of the Agora Preparatory School are probably members of your First Athenian Congregation. If they believe that you know right from wrong, they will have to admit that I, too, am a moral man. I will tell Mel that if he disputes my opinions about religion, he should file a complaint against my evangelical preacher-teacher for corrupting me along with his followers. Yes, I think I shall come to the hearing before the management board as your born-again disciple. Then nobody will dare claim that I am an inventor of new religions."

Upon hearing this, Thrip's face lit up. He assured Socrates it was never too late to save his soul, no matter what he had done before. All he needed to do was to follow Thrip and learn from him. He even broached the idea that upon completing his reeducation, Socrates might appear on Thrip's program as a born-again Athenian. Socrates could present a testimonial to his salvation and endorse Thrip's latest fund-raising drive.

Thrip vowed to make Socrates his student, disciple, and evangelist. Then nobody would dare accuse Socrates of being impious and irreligious! Anyone who accused the Reverend Hugh Thrip or any of his disciples of heresy was a heretic himself! He volunteered to begin Socrates's education immediately. Initially, Socrates could offer 10 percent of his annual salary to the Hugh Thrip First Athenian Congregation, since parting with one's worldly goods is the first step on the road to salvation. To my surprise, Socrates agreed, but he stipulated that first Thrip must teach him the difference between good and evil and right from wrong, and make him into a pious person.

Teacher and student agreed on the terms of Socrates's education. Socrates could ask any question and Thrip would answer, until Socrates finally understood the difference between good and evil. Socrates opened the discussion by asking Thrip for a general definition of good and evil that would allow him to know the morally correct thing to do even in situations that neither he nor anybody else had encountered.

Without any hesitation, Thrip answered. "Good is what I am doing now. Denounce the sinner, may he be a murderer or a disobedient child; whether the sinner is one's own son, or mother, or a complete stranger. Remaining silent and indifferent is evil. Please note, dear Socrates, the hypocrisy of the people who criticize me for denouncing and disowning my son. They claim to believe in the Bible, yet they do not follow its examples. Abraham was ready to sacrifice his son Isaac at God's command. He also abandoned his first son, Ishmael, with his mother in the desert. Does anybody claim that Abraham was anything less than absolutely righteous?"

Socrates seemed impressed and replied, "Dear teacher, I must plead ignorance of matters divine and biblical. Tell me, do you really believe that God brought a flood that annihilated the whole of humanity, save for Noah and his family? Do you believe that God ordered the conquering Israelite tribes to kill all the native Canaanites? Do you think all these things are literally true?"

Thrip again required no time to consider his reply. "Of

course, Socrates! I can tell you not just of the wondrous truths of the scriptures but also of many other things that are not written down and that most people do not know and cannot even imagine, of demons and angels, miracles and curses, and of my own personal revelations and conversations with God and angels that will amaze you."

"I do not doubt that. But perhaps some other time," said Socrates. "Right now, I would like you to give me a clear answer to the question I posed earlier about the meaning of good and evil. You gave me an *example* of what you consider a good action, your disowning of your son. You also presented several examples for actions that you think are evil, such as your son's disobedience in studying an academic subject of his choice and having a girlfriend. But I did not ask you for examples. I requested an abstract *definition* of good and evil, a universal rule or a description of *ideal* forms of good and evil. If we had a rule that distinguished good from evil, we could just apply it to any action we wished to consider and would then know whether it is right or wrong. For example, in the United States it is always wrong to drive on the left side of the street, unless it is a one-way street. If I see a car on the left side of a street I have never driven before, I know the driver—whom I have never met—is breaking the law. Can you please provide me with such a general definition or principle?"

"Of course, Socrates, as you wish. What God likes is good. What God dislikes is evil."

Upon hearing this, Socrates clapped his hands and cried, "Excellent! This is the kind of general definition of good and evil I have been looking for. Whether this definition is true or not is a different matter that we need to examine together next. Let me reiterate your position: An action that God approves of is good, whereas an action that God disapproves of is bad.

Good and evil are opposites because God cannot approve and disapprove of the same behavior in the same context."

"Quite so, Socrates! But remember that it is written that God hates the sin but loves the sinner."

"It is written so indeed. Do you agree with me that this definition of good and evil is useless for believers in many gods—adherents of polytheistic religions? The mythologies of such religions usually tell of the disagreements, struggles, and even wars between gods. Hollywood likes to dramatize them with many special effects. The Greek gods and the gods of German and Indian mythologies became angry and hated each other just like mortal humans. When they could not agree on what was good or bad (ethics); or on what was ugly or beautiful (aesthetics); or on what was just and unjust (political philosophy); they resolved their differences violently. All these disagreements were about values: ethical, aesthetic, or political.

"If a polytheist, who believes in many gods, accepts your definition of good and evil, he or she will lack any direction and be confused. Some gods will approve of an action, and so it will be good according to your definition, while other gods will disapprove of the same action, and therefore it will be bad according to the same definition."

Thrip kissed Socrates on his bald head and exclaimed: "Socrates, my brilliant pupil, you got it! I shall make you a missionary of my church and send you to convert the savage pagans! Would you mind traveling to a place like Papua New Guinea or Los Angeles to spread the word of God? You obviously have a talent for it. I can see you now in my mind's eye: A clearing in the jungle; the pagan chieftains listening to you as you convince them of the moral incoherence and inconsistency of polytheism. Next, they kill all the shamans, slaughter all the witch doctors, burn the temples to their gods, convert, and become moral and pious. You proved what I always say, without one God there can be no right or wrong. As Dostoyevsky put it, if God is dead, then everything may be permitted. Giving the pagans faith in the one and only true God is not just a religious mission to save their souls; it is a moral mission to teach them how to lead a moral life. As you proved, people who worship multiple gods cannot be moral. Without one God there can be no right or wrong."

Socrates gave me the sly smile I last saw when he caught a big fish on a recent fishing trip. "It looks like the monotheistic religions are immune from this kind of internal inconsistency. True, monotheists like Jews, Christians, and Muslims believe in one and only one God who issues directions of what is good or evil, rather than in many gods who disagree about good and evil. But there are several monotheistic religions that disagree about what the one and only God instructs us to do. Even within each religion, there are factions that cannot agree with each other, such as the various branches of Christianity. Within each faction, there can be several feuding leaders and teachings. For example, some television evangelists have had less than complimentary things to say about what you preach and what you have to say about God's will."

. "They were just envious of my success. God talks with me more often than he does with them. God told me that he would forgive them, if they would only get off the airwaves," interjected Thrip.

"Still, different religious leaders have been making radically different claims about what they take to be the will of God. The history of the monotheistic religions is fraught with wars over the correct interpretation of the will of God, of what God approves or disapproves of. Each side thought that the one and only God instructed them to kill and eradicate the other side; they could not all have been right. With monotheism, we indeed solved the problem of the conflicting values of different gods. But we are left with an equally perplexing problem: how to decide between conflicting interpretations of the will of God?"

"This easy question has a simple answer," retorted Thrip. "My own interpretation, of course! I can answer any question you may have about the will of God. If I do not know the answer, I can ask God, God will answer me, and I will pass on the answer to the human race or, at least, to its members who tune into my TV program."

"It may be easy for you, Hugh, if you have direct communication with God. But what about people like me? I do not have God's phone number. God is not on my Facebook® friends list. I do not receive tweets from him. I have to rely on other people for everything I can know of God's will. Each person who talks with God, like you, may feel certain that they are right and the others are wrong. Maybe some of the other people who claim to talk with God but disagree with you are just as honest about what God told them as you are."

"Impossible nonsense! They are false prophets," cried Thrip. "They pretend God speaks to them, but they actually invent what they claim he told them. They just want to get money or power out of their pretensions. They are confidence tricksters!"

"You may well be right, but if God does not tell me directly what is right and wrong or identifies who has the correct interpretation of his will, whom should I believe? How can anyone choose between different interpretations of the will of God, indeed, between different representations of what God holds as good or evil? For example, you decided on an extreme, perhaps irreversible, course of action concerning your son. Can you be sure that you are doing the right thing?"

Thrip was quiet for awhile, taken aback by Socrates's question. He replied, "Surely there are some things, some moral principles, natural laws perhaps that all the monotheistic religions and their interpreters agree on—for example, that murder is evil. Disobeying one's parents is also universally prohibited, I think."

"Indeed, some moral principles like 'thou shall not kill' or the crimes of incest and rape are recognized by all the monotheistic religions and by many pagan religions as well. But many thousands of people have been killed because of religious intolerance among the monotheistic religions; the religions that were involved just disagreed about the difference between murder and justified homicide. The monotheistic religions expanded through such conflicts: most religions were founded and developed in war, then they attempted to encroach on each other during the Crusades, the wars between Catholics and Protestants, the pogroms against the Jews, the recent wars in Yugoslavia, and so on and so on. . . ."

Thrip stopped Socrates abruptly. "Yes, but you are judging people who lived in different cultures according to your own worldview and system of values. Believers did not consider themselves to be committing murder. The crusaders, for example, thought they were liberating the Holy Land from infidels and fulfilling the will of God. They did not think they were murdering people because of religious intolerance, as we may think today."

"Exactly, my dear Hugh," said Socrates. "Though all the religions prohibit murder, they cannot agree on the meaning of murder. Even though everybody agrees that God regards murder as a sin, they disagree about what murder means. When it comes to less obvious cases, such as the unfortunate situation you have with your son, there is no agreement at all. Can you prove that God or at least all religions agree that your son's disobedience is evil and that he deserves to be expelled from your family and congregation? If you can prove that, I shall be your pupil and praise you on your TV program. If you can cure my moral ignorance, I shall testify to the whole world that you performed a philosophical miracle and that I am cured of the chronic ignorance and doubt that have plagued me since childhood."

Hugh Thrip wiped his brow. His plate was empty, and he asked for the bill. He said that he would like to explain clearly to Socrates why good and evil can be reduced to what God approves and disapproves of. Indeed, he was as certain as ever of the identity between good and what God approves of, and evil and what God disapproves of. He also maintained his certainty that his son became evil and had to be punished. But he admitted that he found it difficult to explain why he was so certain of what seemed obvious to him. Since I was fascinated by the conversation and did not want Thrip to give in just as Socrates backed him into a corner, I suggested that we rest for awhile and meet later for dinner at a Greek tavern. Thrip probably did not want to lose face, and so he agreed. As he was leaving, I was happy that at least we postponed the filing of his complaint against his son. If Socrates could make him reconsider over dinner the moral correctness of his actions, perhaps we could still save Thrip's family.

GOD AND ETHICS

That evening, after several combination platters of souvlaki with tzatziki, gyros, moussaka, Greek salad, goat cheese, and different types of olives, it was time to reopen the discussion. Thrip had strong Greek coffee with sweet halva and baklava, and Socrates had several glasses of Metaxa.

Socrates began the conversation. "Suppose you are right that actions God loves are good, while actions God hates are evil. I want to ask you an extremely important question, a question on which the very existence of an independent field of ethical inquiry depends: does God love a good action *because* it is good, or is an action good *because* God loves it?"

"I do not understand your question, Socrates," replied a perplexed Thrip.

"Let me restate the question more clearly then. You know of love and marriage, horse and carriage, engine and car, locomotive and train, and so on. One thing moves or pulls the other thing; one unit leads and the other follows. In each of these pairs, one part is active and the other is passive. Love leads to marriage, the horse pulls the carriage, the engine drives the car, and the locomotive moves the train."

"Sure, I understand you. This is simple."

"Good. Now, let's think of love, such as the love you may feel toward a book, a dish, a movie, or a person like your son. Such love has two components: the subject that loves, which is you, and the object that is being loved, which is your favorite book or dish. Of the two parts of love—the subject that loves and the object that is being loved—which part is the active part (the engine) and which part is being moved (the car)? If you love a book, which is the active part and which is the passive? Do the qualities of the book—how interesting, how well written, and so on—make it loveable, or is it your love of the book that makes it loveable? If a dish like the moussaka you just ate is loveable, is it because it is tasty, well-cooked, made of good ingredients, and so on, or does your loving it makes it loveable?

Now remember what you said a moment ago about right and wrong, about the principles of ethics. You said that God prefers them—fine; we agree. But you left unclear whether you think that the principles of ethics are correct because God prefers them, or whether God prefers them because they are correct. For example, is it wrong to murder just because God says so, or does God say 'thou shall not kill' because it is wrong to kill our fellow human beings and God expresses a negative judgment of murder, just as any intelligent moral being would, irrespective of their knowledge of God's will? Are good deeds intrinsically good and therefore God loves and approves of them, or is the love God has toward these rules the reason for them being considered good? Do the commands of God resemble the command of a mother to her child not to put his hand in boiling water—a good command that the mother endorses out of love for the child, or do the commands of God resemble those of a military officer who should be obeyed by his soldiers because he is their superior officer, regardless of whether or not his commands make any sense? Do you understand this distinction now, Hugh?"

Thrip nodded hesitantly, slowly drinking his coffee. He stared up at the ceiling, as if looking for an answer from above. But Socrates continued relentlessly. "You see, this is the foundation of the distinction between ethics and religion. Both may instruct us similarly not to kill and not to steal and to help old ladies across the street. But ethics attempts to discover the general rules that decide what is good and what is bad, what we should and should not do, with or without a revelation of God's ethical preferences, whether or not we can know them. If ethics does not have to be based on religion, it may distinguish good from evil by using its own methods. We may discover what is good and evil without having to choose between conflicting religious opinions and practices and without having to rely on the kind of revelations that you claim to experience.

"If, by contrast, murder is evil only if God says so, it is impossible for anybody to know what is good and what is evil unless God reveals it. Where do you stand on this matter? Do you think that good or bad acts are good or bad by themselves and that is why God approves or disapproves of them, or are acts good or bad because God approves or disapproves of them?"

"Socrates, I am bewildered. As soon as I am confident of one of the two options, it dissolves, and the alternative appears to be superior. I still feel that I know the answer, but I cannot articulate it. At times, it seems to me that I manage to arrange all my ideas like obedient and well-trained soldiers in one line, single-file, ready to defend their positions and attack and defeat the enemy. The next moment, all my idea soldiers defect in different directions, my front line is in tatters, and I lose the battle before it begins."

"What you have just said demonstrates rare intellectual integrity," praised Socrates. "Had I been saying what you have just said, the parents of my students would have told me that this is the result of being unpatriotic, of demoralizing my ideal philosophical soldiers. But since you admit that the ideal soldiers who defect are yours, you cannot blame me. Your own soldiers defect from your camp."

"But Socrates, my soldiers are not deserting their positions because of weak leadership. They desert because you keep luring them away. Without you, they would have remained loyal."

"And never realize that their line is indefensible?" asked Socrates. "I win wars of ideas without moving any of my soldiers, indeed without having an army at all, merely by exposing the weaknesses in the positions of my opponents, who then realize the indefensibility of their line and retreat without a fight. But enough of metaphors. They get in the way of my education. I am still very keen on being instructed by somebody as wise as you. We should not give up before you are finally successful in teaching me something!"

PIETY

Socrates ordered more goat cheese to go with his brandy and shifted the discussion to a different topic. "Let me raise another, maybe easier question that you are most certainly qualified to answer. There are several religious virtues, like devoutness, piety, and righteousness. I would like you to explain them to me. In particular, I want to know your opinion about the relationship between the practice of these religious virtues and justice. There are three possible answers: First, religious virtue may be a part of justice in general and then all the religious virtues are just. Second, piety, like table manners, may have nothing to do with justice or injustice. Third, some of the religious virtues may be just while others would be neither just nor unjust."

Instead of answering, Hugh Thrip ordered some more Greek sweets. So Socrates gave it another try. "Imagine all the furniture in the world, the *set* of all the furniture in the world. All the chairs in the world are included within this set because all chairs are furniture, but not every piece of furniture is a chair. A table, for example, is a piece of furniture that is not a chair. By contrast, the set of all the stars in the universe has no member, no star that is also a piece of furniture; the two groups have nothing to do with each other. But the set of all the books in the world partly coincides with the set of all the furniture in the world because some books are pieces of furniture; some rich but uneducated people buy them by color and size so they fit the color and shape of their couches. Such people do not care for the content of the books they buy, for they never read them. Other books, hopefully most books, are not pieces of furniture, and most pieces of furniture are not books, so these two sets only partly coincide. Now consider the set of all the just acts and the set of all the religiously virtuous acts, and then try to consider their relationships."

Instead of answering directly, Hugh Thrip imitated Socrates's faux-ignorance methodology by asking him for his opinion. Socrates answered that he thought that the group of religiously virtuous acts was wholly contained within the group of just acts. Every religiously pious or righteous act is also a just act, though not every just act is also pious. Thrip agreed.

Socrates seemed relieved that they reached such an early agreement. He asked then if the Reverend Thrip could teach him more about religious virtue and piety. For example, what part of justice do they occupy? What is their relationship to justice in general? Socrates was particularly eager to learn about religious virtue from Thrip's teachings because he foresaw that Mel Etuxor and his allies would accuse him before the management board of the Agora Preparatory School of being impious and devoid of religious virtue. When that accusation surfaced, declared Socrates, he would be ready, having been schooled about religious virtues by the highest authority. He would prove that it was his accusers who were ignorant of religious virtue, not him, because he was the student of the great Reverend Thrip.

Socrates's unfettered admiration, respect, and earnest desire to learn from him seemed to relax Thrip. He grew confident as he explained patiently, "Look here, Socrates. If I want to define justice in general, as you asked of me earlier, I would say that justice is *proper care*. We care for other people, ourselves, or the world. Each object of care has a form proper to it. These are all forms of justice. For example, we care for our children properly in a different way than we care for our parents properly. The part of justice that instructs us how to care for God properly is religious virtue. Piety, righteousness, devoutness, and so on are all forms of care for God. The other parts of justice instruct us on mostly how to care properly for other human beings."

Thrip reclined back in his chair and stretched his legs. "You have to admit this time, Socrates, I've got it right, just as you asked me. I gave you a clear and elegant abstract definition, as you requested."

"Well done indeed!" exclaimed Socrates. "You expressed your position well and offered the kind of universal rule I asked for. This is almost perfect. I just need you to clarify for me a point or two that I still do not quite understand. Will you be patient with me?

"It is not entirely clear to me what you mean by care. The ordinary use of the word *care* does not seem to fit exactly religious virtue. We say that a car mechanic cares for cars by inspecting them, replacing worn parts and oiling the rest. Are you sure that the practice of religious piety is care for God in a comparable sense? Let us consider what is common to all the types of care we can think of. The breeder who cares for horses aims to improve the horses in a way that benefits them and makes them better than they were prior to being taken care of. Likewise, a car mechanic aims to benefit the car by maintaining and contributing to its smooth operation. Health care aims to benefit the health of its recipients. Caring for children and the elderly also aims to benefit them, either by educating them and making sure they eat properly and so on, or by making sure they receive the best health care available and helping them to avoid the sort of activities that may harm them. We can conclude, then, that care always aims to benefit its object and never aims to harm it. If piety, devoutness, and so on, expressed in worship, are care for God, they must somehow benefit God and make God better than he was prior to being taken care of by the worshipper. Do you think that when you pray, you make God better?"

"Heaven forbid! This is blasphemy. Of course not," cried

Hugh Thrip. "I did not mean what I said, and I did not say what I meant. Of course God is already perfect and God does not need us. There is nothing we can do to improve or benefit God. Let me offer a revised definition: The care we give to God resembles the service that slaves render to their master; a service rather than a benefit."

Socrates considered Thrip's second "care as service" definition of religious virtue. He enumerated types of service. "What is common among car service, service at a restaurant, and national service? All these services achieve a goal, such as the functioning of the car, a good dining experience, and national security. What can be God's purpose then? God must have a purpose for which the pious are used as servants."

"God has many purposes. Since God works in mysterious ways, we do not always know God's purpose or even his means," came the well-recited answer. "I can tell you some wonderful and encouraging stories about his mysterious ways, miracles and wonders that happened to members of my congregation and even to television viewers who touched the screen while I was preaching or anointed themselves with holy waters that I sent them—"

"Some other time, perhaps," interrupted Socrates. "Politicians also have many purposes, and they operate often behind closed doors in what may appear to outsiders as mysterious ways. Still, we can say that they aim to gain or maintain power by being elected. Financial managers have many purposes and work in what many people regard as mysterious ways, still we know they aim to buy equities such as stocks or bonds when their price is low, sell them when their prices rise, and make a profit on the difference between the two prices. How would you sum up similarly the many good purposes of God that the pious serve?"

"As I told you, Socrates, these matters are very difficult. Even people blessed with a special relationship with God, like me, cannot know God's ultimate purpose. But for simple people like you, I would say that if a person belongs to a religious congregation, prays and worships regularly, listens to my sermons, follows my teachings, and makes personal offerings in the form of financial pledges to my ministry, that person is pleasing to God. These are pious acts that could prevent personal calamities and forestall national disasters."

Socrates made sure that his wallet was still in his pocket as the waitress brought the bill. He said, "I expected you to provide a concise definition. If you wish to teach students like me, you have to be precise and to the point. You almost managed to actually teach me something, but you stopped just when it was getting interesting. Instead, you lead me now in a different direction. But as your student, I must follow your guidance. You claim that religious virtue amounts to the knowledge of how to make financial offerings to your church and how to pray?"

"No, Socrates, once again you misunderstand what I said," protested Thrip. "Making a financial pledge is a sacrifice to God through me. When my followers pray, they do not pray to me but through me to God. I am a conduit between them and God."

"No doubt you pass on the donations to God and plead with him on behalf of all the wretched souls who send you their prayers," retorted Socrates. "But I would like to ask you, how does begging God for things we want and making financial sacrifices constitute service to God? You present our relationship with God as a kind of trade, we give God presents and prayers, and God gives us what we want in return. I agree that there are many blessings that we could receive from God. But what exactly can God wish to receive from us?"

"Do I have to repeat myself, Socrates? God receives honor,

reverence, and, above all, gratitude and praise for all the miracles and blessings we receive from him every day."

"So, dear Hugh, religious virtue is the performance of things that are *pleasing* to God, not things that *benefit* God, as you said earlier."

"I think that religious virtue is the practice of all the things that are dear to God," reiterated Thrip.

"But my dear Hugh, you have just returned us to the beginning of our discussion. We have argued in a circle and gotten nowhere. We started this discussion when I asked you for the distinction between good and evil. You proposed that good acts are loved or approved of by God, while bad ones are not. I showed that it is difficult to surmise what God may love or disapprove of because of the great diversity of conflicting representations of the will of God. Then I asked you whether God loves good acts because they are good, or whether these acts are considered good because God loves them; we left the matter alone because you could not answer the question. Now you have returned to your original answer. For the love of God, do you remember? We suggested earlier that good actions, including pious deeds, may not be reducible to what God loves. You display a rare talent for moving around while staying put. We traveled round and round and ended up exactly where we started."

"Alas, Socrates. Our argument has indeed moved in a circle," admitted Thrip.

"Nevertheless, Hugh, I still want to learn from you. Let us not give up!" persisted Socrates. "Let us begin again at the beginning: What is religious virtue? What is good and evil? You must know the answer! If you did not know it for sure, you would not have attempted to disown your own son or ask your church to expel him for disobeying you and for having a Methodist girlfriend. Had you been uncertain of the difference between right and wrong, piety and impiety, you would have been afraid of running the risk of bringing upon yourself the wrath of God if disowning your own son is evil after all. You would have been ashamed of what other people may say about such a cruel condemnation. So, dear Hugh, please tell me and do not prevaricate, what is good and evil?"

Thrip raised his hands in exasperation. "Socrates, it is getting late and I need to prepare a sermon. I shall teach you more some other time. May God be with you and bestow his blessings upon you and cure you of all your ailments in body and soul."

"What are you doing to me, Hugh? I thought you were my mentor and we were friends!" cried Socrates. "You leave me here in a state of complete ignorance as you found me. You promised to teach me right from wrong and instruct me in the religious virtues so I can defend myself against Mel Etuxor's accusations before the management board of the Agora Preparatory School. I relied on outwitting him by using all that I should have learned about religion and ethics from the highest authority, the Reverend Hugh Thrip himself! I thought I would not only be able to defend myself and show that I do not invent new religions or debunk old ones, but that I would also become a better person. You are leaving me in the same state of ignorance as you found me, friend!"

Hugh Thrip got up, shook our hands, thanked me for taking care of the bill, and left the restaurant. I never saw him again and did not learn whether he filed the complaint against his son, and if so, whether he convinced the First Athenian Congregation's council of elders to expel his son, despite all the doubts Socrates had raised.

Regardless of whether we saved Thrip's family, I do not think Socrates debated him in vain. Neither one reached any positive conclusions about good and evil and the nature of the religious virtues. But Socrates came to two important and definite philosophical conclusions: First, he established the independence of ethics and morality from religion when he indicated that God approves of good acts because they are good, rather than good and evil being determined by his will. It is not necessary to belong to a particular religious community or faith to know good or evil. There are many Christians, Jews, Muslims, and pagans who behave morally. Atheists are as capable of doing good deeds and distinguishing between good and evil as anybody else. Philosophers who study ethics attempt to find what is good without any particular reliance on a religious tradition and can themselves belong to different religious communities or to none. Socrates indicated that their search for the discovery of what is good is possible.

Second, Socrates and Hugh Thrip agreed that the religious virtues are parts of justice. This implies that if a religious person is pious and devout, that person cannot behave unjustly. A God who instructs his followers to act unjustly—for example, to kill—is a false God and his prophets are false prophets. God does not require our services or care. If there is a God, he requires us to be just to our family, to our community, and to our fellow human being. Thrip's intended course of action against his son was unjust and therefore could not have been pious. Mel Etuxor's plan to dismiss Socrates from his teaching position was unjust and therefore could not have been motivated by piety.

Soon after this discussion with the Reverend Hugh Thrip, Socrates came before the management board of the Agora School, where he acted in his own defense.

4

YOUR CHILDREN WILL CONDEMN YOU

Socrates's Defense Speech (After the *Apology*)

Socrates was suspended from his high school teaching job at the Agora Preparatory School in rural Virginia following accusations made against him by the parents of three students at the school. They accused Socrates of corrupting his students, of inventing new religions and teaching them to naive kids who trusted their charismatic teacher, and of atheism. The management board of the school, composed of parents, the headmaster and senior management, alumni, and prominent donors and supporters, met to consider the allegations and what to do about them. First, Socrates's accusers presented their charges and attempted to substantiate them. Then Socrates was given the chance to defend himself. I was in the audience with several other friends of Socrates, along with parents, students, and teachers. Due to the large number of people present, the school was forced to use its assembly hall for the meeting.

When his turn came to speak, Socrates stood up to address his accusers and the board. "I cannot know the effect of my accusers' speech on you, how convincing you found them. But I can tell you that I myself was so persuaded by their speech that I almost forgot who I am. Still, there is no truth to their accusations. Of the many falsehoods they told, one stood out, not because it is more false than the others, but because of its brazenness. It was the warning that since I am one of the most eloquent people alive, you should be careful not to be persuaded by my rhetorical tricks. Shame on them for making such a claim! As will become evident momentarily, I am a dreadful lecturer. I have no rhetorical skills. I concede, though, that I do have one—but only one—great advantage over my opponents in this debate: I speak the truth. As you will hear, when I speak the truth, it is unadorned, devoid of stylistic flourishes, rhetorical devices, catchy one-liners, or rhyming jingles. At this advanced stage in my life, it is beneath my dignity to attempt to be an amateur politician, to attempt to play on and manipulate your emotions, or to try to catch you off guard, turn off your reason and critical faculties to smuggle into your mind the message I wish to implant there. I intend to tell you the plain truth, the whole truth, and nothing but the truth.

"You have just heard a series of accusations against me. But these accusations were spoken against a background of rumors, whispers, biases, and prejudices that have been circulating in this country for a long while. If I wish to dispel the new, second set of accusations you have just heard, I had better first demonstrate how incredible they are by making the implicit accusations explicit and rebutting them one by one.

"You must have heard rumors about me. I have been the subject of ridicule for years by talk-show hosts, satirists, stand-up comedians, and YouTube® videos. The only thing these clowns share is ignorance of philosophy in general and of my philosophy in particular. They have been using two cartoon-like stereotypes to augment the comic effect and to save their audiences from having to understand a difficult character and his philosophy. First, they misrepresent me as a kind of mad scientist who has crazy and dangerous ideas and whose inquiries into esoteric subjects may undermine society as we know it. Second, they misrepresent me as a kind of fast-talking slick lawyer or salesperson who can convince anybody of anything. Then, they accuse me of teaching others to become dangerous mad scientists who are also slick lawyers who work for whoever pays them the most so they can prove to any jury that day is night and night is day. I am worried that you have heard such stereotypes and rumors when you were too young to consider them critically. These malicious rumors generated by envious ignoramuses have become entrenched beliefs that are simply false.

"You may remember the Broadway production of a play called *Skyscrapers*, in which a character named Socrates climbed up high-rises, attempting to study the stars and then trying to use antigravity to float between them. What a metaphor for philosophers who float above reality and walk on air! Very funny; I can hardly contain myself. If one of you could bring a rake to scratch me under my armpits, I will also laugh. With all due respect to natural scientists, mad or mundane, I am not a natural scientist. I have nothing to say about nature or its empirical study.

"The misrepresentation of me as a philosopher who can invent an argument for anything if the right financial or material incentive is available is just as false. I do not deny that there are academic philosophers who sell their skills to the highest bidder. They begin their careers in graduate school and choose a department with a good track record for placing its graduates in good jobs. They then choose a dissertation topic and director that are fashionable, irrespective of what they know to be important and true. The philosophical opinions they defend in their dissertations are the same as the ones they expect to land them a job. They are careful to echo the opinions of their fashionable dissertation director. They may summarize and rephrase them. They may then put them in context by comparing them with the positions of other philosophers. They can try to expand their applications to other philosophical subfields, and even rebut criticisms that were leveled at those positions, just as long as they do not dare to express any original thought of their own that may not be sufficiently fashionable. Once they obtain that desirable tenure-track job in a decent department, they are careful not to contradict the professors who will vote whether to grant them tenure. They will not publish anything outside the field they were hired to teach and will avoid displaying any originality. They will inflate the grades of the students who pay, regardless of their performance, and make their dean happy. Then they will finally receive tenure, the kind of job security that will allow them to conduct research on whatever they want, publish their true positions, and give students honest evaluations of their work, even when it is not so good. But by that time, they have nothing to say. Whatever philosophical authenticity, curiosity, originality, and integrity they may have possessed before they passed through the academic mill are gone. They will continue to follow prevailing fashions and echo whatever is being said in the wealthiest and most powerful departments long after the career and economic incentives and sanctions, financial rewards, and threat of unemployment have receded. I am very happy for such professors of philosophy. It is great that they get parents to pay them hundreds of thousands of dollars for this kind of education. I suppose the parents believe it is worth the money they pay, especially if it gets their children to law school, where they can be trained to argue (for a hefty fee) the cases of both the innocent or guilty. But I am a philosopher, not an academic, and I am certainly not a successful and fashionable academic philosopher.

"I guess some people must think that where there is smoke, there is fire. If so many people accuse me of so much nonsense, there must be something behind it. If I were like other people, I would not have gotten into so much trouble. There must be something strange about me. Why do so many people dislike or even hate me?

"I think this is a fair question, and I will do my best to explain to you at length how I acquired my present reputation. Please bear with me. You may think I am joking, but I swear to you that I am about to tell you the whole truth.

"I admit that I am wise. But I possess in abundance only a particular type of wisdom. What kind of wisdom do I have? Here I have to tell you a true story about my childhood. I was not a very good student in high school. I was also very awkward. Nobody knew what was wrong with me, so they sent me to see a psychologist. The psychologist subjected me to a barrage of tests and evaluations and then pronounced to the surprise of everybody, including me, that I was not only the wisest boy in the school but the wisest in the country. My results were just off the charts. It made my father proud for once, and my mother also believed the psychologist.

"Why am I telling you this story? Because therein lies the origin of my bad reputation. When I heard the psychologist's evaluation, I wondered for a long time what it meant. I knew I had no wisdom. The psychologist could not be lying; it was her job to offer an honest evaluation, and she subjected me to the best tests available. I thought about it for a long time and finally came up with a method for testing the psychologist. If I could find somebody who was clearly smarter than me, I would prove that the psychologist was wrong. So I sought out the person with the best reputation for being smart: a world expert on geopolitics. I went to a conference where she gave a paper and then discussed world politics with her after the lecture. I could not help noticing during the conversation that the expert was not really wise; she was just suggesting all sorts of scenarios that other people were too afraid to contemplate, but they were not well-thought-out or supported by evidence. Still, this person was considered wise by other people and even more so by herself. So I attempted to explain to her that although she considered herself very wise, she really was not. As a result, she began to hate me, and that hostility was shared and spread by all the students and colleagues of this geopolitical expert who were present at that conference. So I went away. I concluded, however, that although neither of us understood much about geopolitics or social science in general, I had the advantage of knowing that I do not know, whereas this so-called expert deluded herself into thinking that she possesses special knowledge that makes her an expert.

"I went on to talk with other professional experts: economists and financial portfolio managers, psychotherapists and politicians, climatologists and nutritionists. I reached the same conclusion with all of them. I was wiser than them because I knew they knew nothing about where the economy was heading, which stocks would rise in value, how to cure mental pain, which policy is best for the country, how and why the weather changes, and what kind of diet can prevent Alzheimer's. My only advantage over them was that I knew that I did not know, whereas they mistakenly assumed that they knew things that, in fact, they did not know.

"As I went on talking with these experts of good reputation, I became increasingly aware of the hostility my questioning and doubts were garnering, but I could not stop myself. Like the little boy in the fairy tale about the emperor's new clothes, I was compelled to pronounce the emperor again and again to be stark naked. I discovered that some of the people held in the highest repute were the most foolish, while some people at the bottom of the social ladder were wiser and morally superior.

"After talking with the professionals and the politicians and the high and the mighty, I spoke with artists, poets, playwrights, novelists, and painters. I presented them with some of their most highly appreciated works and asked them to explain their deepest meaning. I thought that artists should be wise about their own creations. But believe it or not, I was wrong. The interpretations given by high school students about these ingenious works were deeper than their own understanding of what they had achieved. This experience proved to me that great artists are creative not because they possess some special wisdom but because they have some genius, inspiration, and talent, which they neither understand, control, nor teach, except for some very particular techniques. Nevertheless, successful artists fancy themselves to be wise in general and offer their opinions on a wide range of topics they know nothing about, from astrology to faith healing, and politics to economic policy. So I left the artists with the same sense of intellectual superiority: I was wiser than them in knowing I was not wise. They were deluded about their own wisdom.

"Finally, I talked with people who had technical knowledge: plumbers and engineers, people who work in hardware stores and professionals who fix things for a living. I was not disappointed, because they did know many useful things that I did not know. In that respect, they were indeed wiser than me. But then they made the same type of mistake as the artists did; since they knew how to fix mechanical systems, they reasoned that they also knew how to fix the greater ills of society and culture, things they knew nothing about. Their illusionary political 'wisdom' tended to be at the opposite end of the spectrum to those of the artists, but both groups fooled themselves into thinking that they possessed political wisdom. I compared myself with the technicians and considered whether it was better to have their limited technical wisdom and the delusion that they are wise about a broad range of higher matters, or whether it was better to be as I was, ignorant but wise in being aware of my ignorance. I concluded it was better to be as I was, aware of my severe limitations but making no mistakes born of delusions of knowledge and wisdom.

"When people attribute wisdom to me, this is the only wisdom I have: I know that I do not know. I am aware of my own ignorance, whereas people who are less wise than me do not know how ignorant they are. I have lived my life in this ignorance, while I keep trying to find somebody wiser who may instruct me and make me wise. Whenever somebody new acquires a reputation for wisdom or expertise, I approach them to see if I can finally find somebody wiser than me. As you can imagine, this way of life has made me many enemies. Nobody likes to discover that they are not as wise as they imagine themselves to be. Professionals and experts depend on public perception of and trust in their wisdom for their income. I have been questioning the social hierarchy that justifies distribution of power and wealth by perceptions of distribution of wisdom. It is no surprise, then, that I have no place in the social hierarchy and that I am poor. While I know many people who have power and money, none are my friends. Many managers do not like an employee who constantly questions the wisdom of their boss and even exposes their stupidity to their colleagues and other employees. I could become an entrepreneur or a politician, but then I would have to lie about my own lack of expertise and spend time on pursuits other than searching for knowledge. I prefer to live in wise poverty.

"One more thing has contributed to my notoriety: the rich kids. Upper-class kids with plenty of time on their hands have attached themselves to me. They like to hear me interrogate established figures and prove to them that they are not as smart as they imagine themselves to be. It appeals to their rebellious nature, at least until they grow up and join the establishment. They are also curious and are still interested in philosophical problems about knowledge, truth, and justice. Since they have rich parents, they do not have to worry about practical, employable skills or work, and they have the time to spend on philosophy. They admire me as being something between a curiosity and a celebrity, and then they imitate me. They begin to question the rationality of hierarchies and the wisdom of authorities. The powerful and rich experts whose ignorance my young followers learn to question are annoyed, but instead of blaming the young people who do the questioning, they blame me, their model. They accuse me of leading their children astray. They do not know and cannot explain what it is that I am teaching to their children that they find so objectionable. So, in bewilderment, they just repeat the same nonsense that everybody else says about philosophers in general and me in particular, that I am some kind of a mad scientist, a slick lawyer type, and—since they associate religion with legitimizing authority, hierarchy, and power—an atheist who teaches their children to doubt traditional organized religion. Since they resent their children for finding out that they have no wisdom, they become aggressive and relentless in destroying my public image. They have been brainwashing the public with loud, ridiculous, and libelous lies about me.

"The group of parents who prosecutes me here decided to gang up on me on behalf of all the financial advisers, lawyers, politicians, artists, religious leaders, and engineers I have ridiculed over the years. I know I cannot expect you to overcome prejudices against me that were instilled over years in one day. I can only tell you the plain and whole truth and hope it convinces you.

"Now let me address the concrete accusations made against me by Patriotic and Good Mel Etuxor, as he likes to call himself. What does he add to the traditional accusations against me? Something like this: Socrates does evil and corrupts his students. He does not believe in traditional religion, and he invents a new religion with new gods. I will argue that Mel and his friends are the doers of evil, not me. He is evil insofar as he ridicules and makes a joke of serious matters. He wastes your time, bringing spurious accusations that revolve around issues he knows nothing about and has no interest in."

Socrates called to Mel, who was sitting opposite him, to answer a few questions. "Mel, would you describe yourself as a person who cares about education, as an educational reformer even, striving to improve today's younger generation?"

Mel answered in the affirmative.

Socrates proceeded. "You claim to know who the corruptor of youth is, and you accuse and prosecute him here. But can you tell us who the reformers of youth are, the great educators who improve their students?"

Mel smiled but did not reply.

"You have nothing to say, Mel? If you are interested in education and care for the improvement of youth, rather than just looking to find some victim for your zealotry, please tell us who should be educating young people?"

"The Constitution!" replied Mel, after some hesitation.

"But the Constitution is not a person, it is not an educator, it cannot stand in front of a class and lead a discussion or ask questions. You mean a person who is well-versed in the Constitution?"

"Everybody here," answered Mel. "Every upright citizen knows the Constitution. Every patriotic parent in this school, every teacher, every alumnus of this school, and every priest, parson, and preacher."

"Do you mean each and every one of them or only some citizens, parents, and so on?" Socrates asked.

"I mean each and every one of them. We are blessed to have so many constitutional patriots in our midst." Mel bowed and smiled in the direction of the school's management board.

"If each and every person here is a constitutional patriot, as you put it, the only exception must be me. I must be the only corruptor of youth around, yes?"

"Exactly! You, Socrates, are the only one. You do not belong here. You should leave or be made to leave this school and return to wherever you came from."

"How very unfortunate for me, if you are right, that I am the only sinner in Sodom, or is it the other way round? Let's talk of horses then. How do people benefit horses by training them? Are well-trained horses educated by constitutionally patriotic horse breeders, and can a single corruptor ruin all that training; or are they trained by a single or at most a few trainers and so can be corrupted by everybody else? What, you have no answer?"

Mel did not react. He stayed seated, simpering and staring in the general direction of Socrates, without quite looking at him.

"Your silence only goes to show how long you have been thinking about education and how ready you are to discuss educational policies and philosophy. Let me ask you something easier: is it better to live among good citizens or among bad citizens?"

Mel kept his gaze focused somewhere above Socrates and did not react.

"Still too difficult for you, Mel? Let us try something easier then. If you have good neighbors, would that benefit you? And if you have bad neighbors, would that harm you?"

Mel mumbled something that sounded like an assent.

"So tell me, is there a single human being who wants their neighbors to harm them? Come on, old buddy, tell me. Does anybody want to be injured?"

"No, nobody," conceded Mel with a sigh.

"To be clear about your accusations, do you think that when I corrupt the youth, I do so intentionally or unintentionally?"

"Intentionally. You want them to be corrupt like yourself," answered Mel without hesitation.

"But then my behavior must be insane. We agreed that good neighbors do their neighbors good, and bad neighbors harm them. If I corrupt the youth, I must be creating bad neighbors for myself who would then harm me. Why should I want to do such a thing on purpose? Do I have a reason to intentionally harm myself? This is as irrational as your accusation.

"There are only two alternatives: either I do not corrupt the youth at all and your accusations are groundless; or I do corrupt the youth, but I do so unintentionally and again your accusation that I intentionally corrupt them is false. Incidentally, had my offense been unintentional, the proper course of action would have been to take me aside and explain to me what I was doing unintentionally and suggest remedial action, rather than file a formal complaint with the school board."

Socrates turned to the members of the management board and addressed them directly. "As you must have noticed, Mel could not care less for education or for logical consistency. His accusations are internally inconsistent. They just make no sense."

Turning back to his accuser, Socrates resumed his questioning. "Allow me to ask you again to clarify your accusations.

You accused me of corrupting my students. What is the nature of this corruption? I infer from the text of your complaint that you claim I teach them to reject the traditional religions that have been in practice since the founding of the United States and that fit well with our Constitution, and that instead I try to convince them to join some new religions with new gods and rituals. These new religions I invent or introduce are supposed to corrupt my students, right?"

"Exactly," said Mel emphatically and with disdain.

"Then for God's sake—excuse the pun—please tell us in simple terms, what do you mean? Do you mean that I am a religious person but of a new, nontraditional religion and that I believe in a god or gods, though they are not of the traditional variety; or do you claim that I am an atheist, a person who does not believe in any god? You contradict yourself when you accuse me of both. To be logically consistent, you can only accuse me of one of the two charges. Which one do you choose?"

Mel rushed immediately to claim in an indignant voice that Socrates was a complete atheist of the type who denies all traditional religions and gods.

"How extraordinary, Mel. Whatever makes you say that? Do you mean that unlike most of your friends and relatives, I do not believe that God created the world in six days and that all the species were created in their present immutable shape rather than having evolved from previous forms, that sort of thing?"

"Exactly!" burst out Mel, addressing the management board. "Have no doubt, he believes in none of it. He believes the world started billions of years ago in a burst of energy he calls the big bang. He also believes that species have evolved from others in a process of random genetic mutation and natural selection."

"Stop there, Mel, old buddy. You think you are prosecuting modern science? Are you putting contemporary cosmology and biology on trial? You may want to prosecute, or, failing that, persecute the likes of Stephen Hawking, Richard Dawkins, and Charles Darwin. But may I remind you that I am a philosopher and not a scientist. You are confusing natural history with philosophy. You think the members of the management board of this school do not know that the students here do not need to learn any of these scientific theories directly from me but can instead purchase paperback popular science books for a few dollars at any bookstore or online? If I ever claim that these theories are my own, my students will laugh me out of class. They know about these scientific theories and where they come from.

"This confusion pales in comparison with the very inconsistency of accusing somebody at once of being an atheist who does not believe in any god and of being the inventor and promoter of new religions with new gods or other supernatural deities. Mel is lying, and he must know that he is lying. Like other slanderers, he attempts to throw any dirt he can find at his victim. The fact that the accusations are mutually inconsistent and therefore cannot hold together does not bother him. He hopes that at least one of them will stick in the minds of uncritical listeners. Mel's complaint is nonsense because he has nothing real with which to accuse me. But nobody with any intelligence would ever believe that an atheist is a believer in new religions with new gods.

"I have said enough to refute all of Mel's and his friends' spurious accusations. If I am convicted today, it will not be because of Mel's ridiculous accusations but because my philosophical practice has made me many enemies over the years. People do not like to be made to look and feel stupid; they resent the smart alecks who show it to them. They tell themselves, 'He thinks he is smarter than us; we will show him who is smart around here,' and they reach for a rock or a wooden club to hammer on his head.

"An encounter with a wise and critical philosopher can generate different reactions. Some people, like my young followers, wish to learn from me and even imitate my philosophical practice. Other people become envious. They think that if they eliminate the object of envy, kill him, expel her, make her work in a field in which she is overqualified, make him lose his job because of some ridiculous accusations that no decent person would ever consider or take seriously, they will miraculously become wiser. But this is nonsense. Destroying the wise philosopher is not going to make anybody else wiser, any more than destroying the entrepreneurial rich makes anybody wealthier or defacing a beautiful object makes anybody prettier. On the contrary, destroying the wise person makes everybody less smart because she is not around to criticize them when they are wrong, correct them when she can, and teach them how to be wiser. Still, I am not the first philosopher to be hated and suffer for being wiser than other people, nor is there any danger that I will be the last.

Some of you may ask, If you are so smart, why are you poor? Why have you never obtained for yourself a well-paying academic or other position? Why are you in a position where people like us can decide on your professional fate? Would it not have been better for you at this stage in your life to be in a safe and secure job and not have to face complaints and trials and possible sanctions? Surely, you may say, that had I led a different life, had I not questioned the wisdom of the high and mighty, had I not consequently put into doubt the social hierarchy that is justified by it, had I not questioned the values and beliefs that many people hold sacred, I would not have made myself as many enemies and would not be standing before you here today.

"I think such suppositions are wrong. A good person should not decide whether or not to do the right thing according to how they believe it would affect them. The only relevant criterion is whether or not the action is the right thing to do. Otherwise, there would be no heroes, only idiots who sacrificed or risked their lives with no direct benefit for themselves. People whom we respect, like firefighters, the soldiers in George Washington's army, civil rights activists, and so on, would have been ashamed of themselves if they had acted only for their benefit. They did the right thing. But there was no personal computation that could have led them to behave heroically. Moral life is a bit like war. Your commander stations you where he chooses, and you have to do your best to hold the line, even at the cost of endangering your own life because death must come before dishonor. I am where I am in life, I must hold my line, and I cannot retreat.

"Many years ago, I was a soldier. When I was ordered to hold a line, I held it, facing death. My line now is philosophy, the quest to investigate and know myself and other people. If I deserted my fort now for fear of losing my job, or of poverty, or even of death, things would be very strange indeed. I would have to deny everything dear to me. Everything I have considered wise would have to be unwise, and vice versa.

"Most people think that death is the worst thing that can happen, so they spend their lives in fear of death. But there is nothing wise about fear of the unknown—and that is what death is. Maybe death will be lots of fun. Who can tell? Here my famous Socratic ignorance is another proof of my superior wisdom. Unlike most people, I know that I do not know what follows death, and that death is the worst thing that can possibly happen; it is definitely worse than the threats made by bullies who try to control the behavior of others.

"But here is something I do know for sure: injustice is evil and dishonorable. It is better to choose a possible good over a certain evil, to choose death over injustice. If you gave me a suspended sentence, allowing me to keep my job but forcing me to commit myself to stop all philosophical inquiry, all questioning of authority and critical examination of the alleged wisdom of people on threat of being fired immediately if I reverted to such inquiries, I would thank you politely for the offer and decline it. As long as I am alive and healthy, I will never stop practicing and teaching philosophy or encouraging others to follow my example. I will try to convince anybody to join me, telling them: You are a citizen of the greatest nation this planet has ever seen, the most powerful and the wisest. Why do you care so much about becoming rich, powerful, and famous but care so little about becoming wise, living in truth, and caring for your soul? You spend hours each week at the gym caring for your body, you care about what you eat so it improves rather than harms your physical health, and you visit experts and doctors to maintain your health. But what about your mind? Don't you think that you should exercise it at least as often as you exercise your body? Don't you think you should care about what you "feed" it? Is not a diet of dumb television shows, vampire novels, and easy listening as dangerous to the mind as smoking is to the body? When was the last time you saw a philosopher to examine what goes on in your mind and to discuss the improvement of its health?

"If the person I reproach in this way answers that I am wrong about her because she does care for her soul, I do not let her go, nor do I leave her. I begin interrogating and cross-examining. If I discover that she misrepresented herself and that in fact she does not care about her mind but only says so, then I reproach her for undervaluing what is really important in life and overvaluing what is insignificant. This message is equally valuable to all people, irrespective of age, creed, nationality, domicile, sexual orientation, and shoe size, but it is especially relevant for my fellow Americans, because philosophy is the foundation of our Republic and the civic virtue that supports it. Freedom of speech, the freedom to debate, criticism of the state and of authority, irreverence of established religions are all at the foundation of our democracy. I daresay that few other citizens promote these basic democratic values as well and as extensively as I do, for I do nothing but try to persuade everybody, young and old, to not care about material wealth or personal fame but to care about the improvement of their minds, to care for their souls at least as much as they care for their bodies and their bank accounts. Money cannot buy good character, and good character begets all the real goods. This is what I teach. If this constitutes the corruption of the youth, then, indeed, it is devastating. But if anyone claims that I teach anything else, they are lying.

"Dear members of the management board, acquit me or convict me as you wish, but have no expectation that I will ever change my philosophy, my way of life, or my teachings, even if I have to lose the only source of income for me and my family, and even if I have to die for my love of wisdom."

When Socrates concluded his defense speech in this defiant tone, the members of the board were clearly upset. Like other men in power, they did not like their authority to control and determine outcomes undermined. They would have liked to enjoy the little power they had over Socrates's life and have him beg them to keep his job and offer all sorts of concessions and compromises to assuage them. The best chance he had for keeping his job would have been to admit some guilt, appear penitent, and above all respect the powers of the management board. Instead, Socrates offered no apologies and undermined their authority by explaining to them why their decision did not matter. They had no power, no control, no leverage over him. Offended, they interpreted this as a challenge to their authority, and, like other petty officials jealously guarding their minor powers, they would move to assert that authority. Meanwhile, they broke into conversation with each other, expressing their outrage at Socrates's insolence.

Socrates asked them to hear him out. "Listen to me, because what I am about to tell you will do you a lot of good. I need to tell you one more thing that may make some of you even more upset at me, but I beg you not to be angry. I have to tell you that if you make me lose my job, you will harm yourself much more than you will hurt me. If you attempt to harm me, you will necessarily fail, because by nature, morally inferior people cannot harm the morally superior. I do not deny, of course, that wicked people may cause great injuries to good people. Such people have been killing, torturing, imprisoning, confiscating property, driving into exile, and depriving of rights since the dawn of civilization. Many of their victims have been good people. But although evil people imagine that they do more harm to others than to themselves, they are wrong. They harm themselves far more than they can possibly harm their victims. I argue now not for my own sake but for yours. If you convict me, you will harm yourselves much more than me. I may lose a job, but you will lose your souls. You will be rejecting one of the best things to happen to this school and our democracy, and the values upon which they rely, namely, me. If you fire me, you will not easily find anybody who can replace me. If I may use a funny metaphor, I am a kind of gadfly on the back of this school and society in general. Large, old bureaucratic organizations like the state or this school are like a hippopotamus that can hardly move because they are so big and fat. They require something or somebody to make them move, or they will remain mired in a swamp, splashing water on themselves but doing nothing. I am a kind of gadfly that makes such bureaucracies move, for I constantly sting, bother, complain, reproach, raise issues, criticize, subject to critical analysis, ask questions, moralize, teach, suggest alternatives, and attempt to persuade. I am so good at being a gadfly that I do not think you will find another one to replace me. Good gadflies are really hard to come by. They are sensitive little insects. It is very easy to swipe at them, but then others will not come.

"I would advise you, then, to give me a break and leave me in peace. You may feel annoyed when you slumber there in the swamp and I suddenly sting you to awaken you into action. You may delude yourselves into thinking that if you kill me in one easy slap of your tail that you will be able to go on sleeping for the rest of your lives. But being mired in a swamp is no great fun. Unless fate and chance send another gadfly your way, you may stay there indefinitely.

"I must admit to two more social vices that you may consider adding to all the other personal faults you find in me: I am poor and I lack political connections. I am not an academic, and I have not charged anybody who wanted to learn from me or watch and listen to me philosophizing. I watched dispassionately as my family and I lived in relative poverty. I gave good advice to my fellow countrymen; I tried to make them into better and more moral people. But this is not the kind of job that anybody gets paid for. Consequently, I lack what some call bourgeois respectability. Being paid inappropriately is one charge even my accusers here, who have been picking at straws to find faults in me, have not accused me of.

"I also lack political connections. No senator or governor or even a municipal potentate will call the director of this school or the chairman of this management board to lobby on my behalf, to ask for favors for me, or to make threats to you to leave me alone. I have remained strictly nonpolitical and independent all my life. It may seem curious. After all, I have spent my life discussing public issues and criticizing public figures. So why not step into the public arena, go into politics, and attempt to apply my wisdom to policy issues as a holder of public office? I owe you an explanation.

"You may have heard from my accusers that I hear voices. They mean to ridicule me as insane. But there is some truth to what they say. I have been hearing one voice since I was a child. This voice comes to me and tells me not to do some of the things I consider doing. But it never tells me what to do. Over the years, I decided to name that voice Conscience. I know this voice is quite special since many people obviously hear no such voice. This voice has forbidden me from becoming politically involved. I think this command was wise and smart. I believe that had I entered politics I would have been quickly attacked, marginalized, and eliminated before I'd had the chance to do any good for myself or anybody else.

"No conscientious politician who follows the dictates of justice and his own ethical convictions, fighting the special interests, injustice, and populist policies will survive an election. The special interests will finance his opponents. The established powers who benefit from injustice will attempt to block him and spread negative information about him. The emotional multitudes like and admire politicians who can enflame their passions. To be successful, a populist politician must be able and willing to manipulate strong emotions like fear, hate, envy, and so on. My whole life as a philosopher has been devoted to controlling and suppressing such emotions. It is against my nature and conviction to try to enflame them.

"Not all politicians are evil. Some are not entirely in the

pockets of the special interests, some can resist established unjust powers, and some try not to enflame the worst emotions we possess. But they all have to make compromises on their principles of justice, build coalitions, and commit small injustices in the hope of preventing greater injustices later. They must distinguish means from ends and attempt to apply some calculation to measure the extent to which good consequences are greater than necessary evil means. I am no good at such calculations. I believe in doing the right thing irrespective of consequences. A person such as me is better off doing justice in the immediate realm of his private life, to his family, friends, and compatriots.

"Actions speak louder than words, so let me share with you several episodes from my life that illustrate what I have just explained theoretically. These episodes show that I would never commit an injustice because some authority or another attempts to bully me and threaten me with death. Both happened during my military service. The marines raided enemy positions. The marines won the battle, but then a storm forced them to retreat before they could collect the bodies of their fallen comrades to bring them home for burial. The families of the fallen were furious and demanded that the commanders be punished. Under political pressure, the military formed a tribunal to try them. I was appointed to serve on the jury in that tribunal. The military authorities made it clear that they expected us to convict the sergeants in charge to divert public anger from the higher echelons. I was the only one to refuse to convict. After I cast my vote, I was threatened that if I did not recast, I would be reassigned to a front-line combat unit with the highest mortality rate in the military. I refused to be bullied.

"Later on, as you remember, the war did not go well for our side. In desperation and exasperation, believing that local civilians were assisting our enemies, the military allowed and even encouraged terrorizing civilians. My commanders became involved then in a war crime. They raided a village and killed every living thing in it. Then, because they became afraid of whistleblowers from within the unit, they decided to get everybody implicated in war crimes so they would have as much against those who had not participated in their raid as we had against them. They ordered us to 'clean' another village. I refused to participate in that raid and just went back to my barrack. They threatened me that, during the next battle, they might not cover my back if I did not cover theirs, and they could not guarantee that I would not become the victim of friendly fire. The other soldiers who were ordered to participate in the raid did as they were ordered. Soon thereafter, the officers were relieved of their commissions and eventually tried. I was just lucky to have survived that situation. But had the military authorities delayed their reaction, I could have been killed by those war criminals.

"You can see now why I would not have survived for long in public office. I would have always made the right and honorable decision and taken the right course of action. I would have been lucky to escape the public sphere with my life, let alone my job. The same holds for my dealings with other people. I do not tolerate injustice in other people any more than I do in myself. That includes those whom people consider my pupils. I have no dogma to teach, and therefore I do not consider myself a teacher. There is hardly anything of substance that anybody can claim to have learned from me. Nobody can write a book about the teaching of Socrates. I only ask questions, analyze answers critically, and ask some more questions. People like to watch me ask questions. Some people like to do so more than once. Then other people start calling them my pupils. But I never charge anybody money to listen to me. Nor do I test them to find out how good they have become in following my teachings, because such a test would have no substance; there are no factual answers for what Socrates believes in, with the sole exception that it is better to suffer injustice than to perpetrate injustice. If any of my so-called students did not follow this principle, it is not my fault. As I just said, I do not test, certify, or guarantee anybody as a discipline of Socrates. Nor do I promote any secret or esoteric doctrine imparted to a few select students because I fear for the reaction of the public if it becomes known. There are no secrets in my philosophy. Whatever I said in public is all there is. If anybody attempts to shift to me the blame for something they have done by claiming to follow an esoteric doctrine that I had taught them, they are simply lying.

"People ask: What is the secret of your appeal? How does an ugly old man attract so many beautiful, well-educated young persons from good families? The explanation, as I told you already, is quite simple: no magic is required. I am amusing. Young people resent authority and are curious to find their own path in life. They enjoy my irreverent examination of the alleged wisdom of powerful and respected experts and professionals. What effect I have on them I do not know. But I do know that I do not corrupt them. I have had so many fans over the past three or so decades that had any of them realized later in life that I had had a bad or corrupting influence on them, they—or at least some members of their families—would have accused me by now, like so many former members of cults and their families. Nobody has ever complained about me. On the contrary, in the audience here today I see so many old friends and their family members who came to support and encourage me today. Note that my adversaries have not brought a single witness against me who used to be one of my so-called students or any member of their families. They can still do something about that, if they wish; so many of my admirers and their families are in the audience. But of course they will not dare bring any of them to testify because they would only deny that I have exerted any corrupting influence over them. If allowed to speak, they would only prove that my accusers lie and that I am telling the truth.

"This is pretty much all I have to say in my defense. Allow me just to say something about what I am not going to do to defend myself, because some of you may expect some kind of a performance here, and I will have to disappoint you. I owe you an explanation so that you are not offended. On previous similar occasions, employees facing possible dismissal tried to appeal to the mercy and compassion of the members of the management board. They brought to court their screaming little children and sobbing spouse. Their friends pleaded for mercy. They appeared in tattered tweed jackets, old corduroy pants with holes, and shoes with worn soles that had not been shined in years to emphasize their poverty. They cried and begged to keep their job because they were the only bread-winner in their family, and unemployment would spell doom and gloom for their innocent children and spouse. I am not going to offer any such spectacle. I hope you will not be angry with me for it. I am of course made of flesh and blood, not marble and ice. I do have a family, including three little chil-dren. But you will not see them today, and they will not beg you to have mercy on us. Please do not interpret this peculiar absence as contempt or disregard toward you. Whether or not I am afraid of losing this job is an entirely different issue that I do not consider relevant. The reason I have not invited my family here is because I feel such emotional manipulation is demeaning both to the accused and to the ones assigned to judge him. Self-humiliation does not become somebody with my reputation for wisdom. Whether or not this reputation is justified, everybody clearly believes that I am different from or even superior to the rest of humankind, so allow me to behave differently and superiorly, just as those of you with superior character or honor would not demean yourselves in this way.

"It is difficult for philosophers who lose their jobs to find alternative employment. But it does not justify the moral license some self-designated philosophers have given themselves to act immorally and dishonorably just to gain or keep their jobs. I will not mention how some European academic philosophers debased themselves and their profession by collaborating with some of the worst regimes of the twentieth century to get a promotion and keep their job. Such behaviors have given philosophy a bad reputation. They allow interpretations of philosophy that reduce it to an academic power structure and present philosophers as clowns in the service of tyrants or as paid public relations spokespersons. I am made of a different moral fiber.

"Apart of the honor, authenticity, integrity, and moral fiber of the defendant, it is unjust for any judge in any court or tribunal to decide on a case on the basis of the emotional appeal of the defendant. The moral duty of a judge is to decide each case on its merits and not to do favors or disfavors for the defendant. The verdict should result from laws, rules, and regulations and not from the sympathies of the judges. If I attempted to manipulate the verdict you are about to decide on by using emotional tricks, I would only be providing evidence for the case against me, I would be as corrupt and impious as they accuse me of being. And so I leave it to you and your gods to decide what is best for you and for me."

With these words, Socrates rested his case. The members of the school's management board retired to their office to vote whether or not to convict Socrates. Considering the offensive and condescending attitude many of the managers inferred from Socrates's defense speech, it is surprising that he was convicted by only a small majority.

According to the regulations of the Agora Preparatory School, once a guilty verdict was returned by the management board, the convicted offender had the right to propose his own punishment. If the convicted seemed sufficiently contrite and repentant, and if the board considered the proposed punishment sufficient, the punishment would be enforced. If not, the management board would decide on its own punishment. Socrates could have appeared chastened and contrite, and he could have suggested for himself a mild punishment, such as writing a letter of apology to the managers, accepting limitations on what he could and could not say in and out of class, disowning some of his earlier statements, and offering to take evening classes in pedagogy that concentrated on the virtues and methodologies of learning by rote in contrast to and instead of his famous Socratic dialogues. However, Socrates had another kind of punishment in mind.

"I cannot say that I am surprised at the verdict you reached. I am only surprised at the narrow majority by which you reached it. I had expected an overwhelming majority against me. Had a few votes shifted from one side to the other, I would have won the day. Be that as it may, we have to face the demand of my accusers to dismiss me from my job. I am supposed to propose an alternative punishment, so what should it be? Clearly, I should receive what I deserve. I have never been lazy. I never took a vacation and stopped philosophizing. But I have received little of what others value. I am poor. My family is poor, too. I have never held public office or had any political appointment made through connections. I have not benefited from my fame in some nonmaterial way. The rich kids who come to listen to me do not invite me to their homes or their parties. I have been too honest to become involved in politics or other affairs that people benefit from materially. Instead, I have worked tirelessly to improve you and everybody else. Everywhere I went, I sought to persuade everybody that they should try to know themselves and strive to care for their souls, to be just and wise before caring about private interests. My politics, likewise, put national wisdom and justice first and national interest second. So, what do I deserve for all these services to humanity and our nation? I am a public good that benefits others without being paid, like public highways and libraries or like the national sports team that makes us all proud and happy when it wins. I deserve to be rewarded rather than punished. The reward should fit the benefit I have granted freely to all, something useful for an old man who just wants to have the free time to go on philoso-phizing and encouraging others to do the same. In this school, the most respected students and the most highly paid instruc-tors are in the athletics department. They have their own table in the dining hall where they get oversized portions. I think I am at least as useful for this school as the athletes. I suggest, then, that what I deserve is to receive free meals at the school's dining hall at a table of my own, so that anybody who wishes to talk with or listen to me can do so and also receive a free meal. I think this is just, because the guys from the athletics depart-ment already have enough money and fame, and I have none. The athletic achievements of our teams make you feel as if you shared in their success, but this is only an illusion, since it was not really you who made the touchdown. You could not do it yourself because you do not possess the necessary athletic skills.

But when you become wise with me, you do score a real touchdown. You can care for your souls and become wise just like me. So, to sum up, I suggest that my penalty will be to receive free lunches at the school's dining hall."

Looking at the members of the management board, Socrates could see that they were not amused. His proposal did not go over well with most of them. He did not look surprised but smiled and said, "Perhaps you think I am ridiculing you with this proposal for punishment, just as I laughed off the pathetic displays of misery that other employees in my position have conducted to manipulate your emotions. But let me assure you that I do not intend to make fun of you or this august board. I am simply certain that I have never intentionally harmed anybody. I realize that I did not manage to convince you of that in my previous speech, but I sincerely believe that, had I more time to discuss these matters with you at length and at our leisure in a more relaxed environment, I would have convinced each and every one of you. Please try to understand that since I object to harming anybody, I am not going to propose a punishment to harm myself. If you accept the punishment my accusers propose, I cannot tell if losing my job here will be a good or bad thing. I may find something better to do elsewhere. But if I propose a punishment for myself, it will surely be a bad thing. What kind of punishment could it be? A promise to adhere to lesson plans and stop talking philosophy with my students? An agreement to take so-called pedagogy classes so that some uneducated 'pedagogical expert' can tell me I should not ask questions in class nor let students talk because they cannot learn from each other, and that they can only memorize the highly simplified dictations I give them? A promise not to talk with my students outside of class? I should much rather be dismissed. I know you may find it hard to believe, but I simply cannot stop talking with people, because I believe that the greatest good to myself and others can only come from discussing goodness, the nature of good character, and truth and knowledge and the other subjects that concern me. You may be surprised to hear this, but I believe that an unexamined life devoid of such philosophical discussions and consideration is not worth living. Such a life is nothing but sleepwalking, automatic repetition of patterns of behavior, living the life of a zombie. I know I failed to convince most of you, but this is the truth. I live in this truth and I am ready to die for it."

This time the management board took even less time to reach by an overwhelming majority a decision to dismiss Socrates. When informed of this, Socrates was given the right to address the management board for the last time.

"Your decision today will do much for the reputation of your school. Everybody will know that you dismissed Socrates, the best teacher you ever had and a wise man, though as I told you, I am not wise at all. Your enemies will use it against you. Your decision demonstrates your impatience, for sooner or later, I would have left of my own accord either because I would have received a more interesting offer elsewhere or because age would have taken a toll on my health and I would have had to take things easier and retire. I am addressing now only those of you who voted to dismiss me. I have one other thing to tell you: You probably think that I mishandled my defense, behaving foolishly and wantonly. You probably think that, had I behaved more humbly and addressed you in the pathetic manner you expected—cried and begged and so on—I could have swayed some of the votes in my direction and would have kept my job. But I do not think that keeping a job justifies humiliating or demeaning myself and everything I stand for: philosophy, the virtuous life, wisdom, and all the rest of it. With due respect to

Lenin, ends do not justify, let alone sanctify, means. In life, as in war, there are many ways to stay alive. But not all of them are right and honorable. The difficult part is not to stay alive but to live in the right way. We spend our lives running away from death or other frightful things like unemployment. But we should remember, dear friends, that there are faster runners than either death or destitution that can catch us much more quickly, especially if we cannot see them, such as wickedness and lack of integrity. I am leaving you today having lost my job, but wickedness also leaves here today empty-handed; it did not catch me because truth, honesty, and goodness chased them away. I am happy to report that my spine and moral fiber are all intact. I consider this result acceptable and if not just, just enough.

"Let me make a prediction—call it an educated guess— about what will happen next. After I leave this school and your punishment comes to pass, you will be the recipients of more severe punishments. You are dismissing me because you do not want anyone to criticize you and force you to reflect and think about your own lives and souls. But there will be others who will criticize you, and they will be much more censorious than me. My presence has restrained these critics. But since they are much younger than me, they will offend you much more than I ever did and their judgment of you will be more severe. If you think that by firing one critic you will get rid of criticism, you are about to discover just how wrong you are. This is neither possible nor moral. The easiest and most honorable way is not to bully your critics but to reform yourselves and your institution. Otherwise, your own children will condemn you."

Upon hearing that last comment, most of the members of the management board got up and left the hall. Socrates ignored them and continued.

"Let me address the members of the management board who voted to acquit me, before I leave this building forever. Let those others leave. I have nothing more to tell them. But let us talk with one another for a while, for the last time, before they force us to vacate the building. You are my friends, and I want to discuss with you the meaning of what happened to me today. I can share with you one wonderful and remarkable piece of news. As you know, I have this inner voice within me that I call Conscience that I cannot control. This voice often forbids me from doing or saying things. Sometimes it stops me in the middle of a sentence, and then I cannot continue talking. But today, I have not heard that voice even once. It did not stop me when I walked into this hall this morning. It did not interfere when I delivered my defense speech and offended the managers. It remained silent when I suggested free lunches as an appropriate punishment for my philosophical practice, and it said nothing when I was dismissed from this job. I believe this is a very strong indication that what I have done and said today is unobjectionable, for this inner voice of mine is very strict and demanding, and it intervenes often in my actions to stop me. I think it is also possible that being forced to leave this teaching position is not a bad thing, or the inner voice would have stopped me from bringing it about. Losing this job therefore probably will do me no harm and will quite probably do me much good. If so, I have no reason to be angry with the people who complained about me, accused me, and misjudged me. They have not harmed me substantially, though they have obviously not intended to do me good. Their ill will and wicked intentions should be condemned nonetheless, even though they may not have harmed me.

"Let me ask you for just one favor. When my children grow up, and if, unlike their father, they prefer fortune or fame or power or anything else to caring for their souls, for the sake of goodness and wisdom and truth, please punish them, criticize them, pester them, annoy them, as I have done with the experts, the politicians, and the religious leaders. If they care about anything more than for their souls, especially flashy, shallow things, like physical appearance and money and what other people think about them, please—whether or not I am still around—reprove them to care about what is important. Then you will do justice for me and for my children.

"It is time for me to leave this place and for you to stay here. Who is luckier, I do not dare to speculate."

5

DEATH AND LIBERATION

(After the *Phaedo*)

On Interstate 81, just south of Binghamton, New York, there is a restaurant next to a gas station that you can recognize by the plywood on one side. Graffiti on the plywood reads: "No parking inside restaurant." The restaurant serves minimal fare of sandwiches, burgers, and fries to motorists on their way between upstate New York and the city. The restaurant is completely devoid of any pretension to style, beauty, or sophistication. It sells simple food for reasonable prices to people on the go who prefer a simple and reasonable meal. The more sophisticated travelers drive another five minutes and park outside A Taste of Texas for Southern-style barbeque in the frozen ambience of an upstate New York highway.

In that restaurant, of all places, Fred and Cheryl, two of Socrates's oldest philosophical companions, ran into each other. Cheryl had found work teaching mathematics and philosophy upstate and so had been forced to leave Socrates's immediate social circle in the city. Fred worked until his retirement, building stairways in New York. For three decades, he was a regular among the circle of friends and admirers who surrounded Socrates. He performed hard physical labor during the day and philosophized in the evenings. Some people admired his ability to do both. He claimed to think about philosophical problems while cutting wood and installing stairs. After a stroke from which he eventually recovered, Fred retired but remained in New York.

Upon recognizing Fred, Cheryl invited him to sit with her. Since they were acquainted through their friendship with Socrates, he was the obvious topic of conversation. Cheryl regretted that since she had moved upstate, she was unable to be with Socrates when he died and wondered if Fred had been there. When Fred told her that he had been with Socrates until the very moment of his death, she insisted that he tell her all about the last day of Socrates's life. She wanted to know what Socrates talked about before his death and how he approached it. She had heard, of course, that Socrates chose to die after a long illness. But she did not know any of the details.

Fred asked if she knew that Socrates had been a patient for months at a hospice after he was diagnosed with a form of sclerosis similar to Lou Gehrig's disease. Cheryl acknowledged that indeed she had heard that. She was surprised, since patients usually do not stay for such a long time at a hospice. Fred explained that Socrates surprised the doctors, who did not expect him to survive for as long as he did.

Cheryl wanted to know all the details. If Fred had the time and it was not too painful or personal, how did Socrates die? Who was there with him? Did the doctors allow Socrates's friends to be there?

Fred assured Cheryl that he had all the time in the world. The memory of Socrates and his death was not painful at all. Quite the contrary, it was a pleasure to recall the last conversations he had had with the philosopher. He was especially happy to talk about Socrates with an old friend who also knew him well.

"Socrates died with most of his friends around him. On that

last day, we knew he would die at the end of the day. But we felt no sorrow or regret. This may be surprising to some. Here we were, at Socrates's deathbed, his best friends, yet nobody felt sorry for him. Socrates himself was not sad. He was in a good mood and as talkative as ever. There was no dread or fear of death in his demeanor, though he knew his end was fast approaching. I felt that if there were an afterlife and Socrates would be traveling to that 'other side,' his trip would be direct, smooth, and happy, and he would be well received there. Although I felt no sorrow or pity, I was also devoid of the kind of joy or pleasure that I usually felt at participating in Socrates's philosophical discussions. All of us felt a strange mixture of pleasure and pain: pleasure at doing philosophy with Socrates and pain at knowing this would be our last conversation with him. We laughed and cried at the same time, especially young Apollo, who is very emotional, as you probably remember."

Cheryl smiled, recalling how Apollo cried watching plot twists in soap operas, had second servings of desserts, cheered wildly at sports, and laughed hysterically at any joke. He once publicly contemplated suicide when his romantic advances were rebuffed. Socrates had to convince him it was not worth it.

"How many people were there?" asked Cheryl. "Please let me know all the details of Socrates's last philosophical discussion."

"There were about twenty of us, locals and visitors.

"But I should start at the beginning. Before that last day, we visited Socrates in the hospice every day. We would meet early in the morning just before visiting hours, beginning our discussion in the waiting room, before we were allowed in. Once the doors were opened, we went to Socrates's room and spent the rest of the day with him, until the nurses showed us the way out at the end of visiting hours. On that last day, we met even earlier than usual. The evening before, Socrates had told us that his physical state was deteriorating quickly and his days were numbered. He decided then to end his life the following day, before the disease that gradually paralyzed his body from the bottom up reached his head and his mind.

"This day, when visiting hours started, the orderly asked us to wait, explaining that Socrates was in consultation with his doctors. After the meeting was over, we entered Socrates's room and saw that he had just been disconnected from the infusion tubes that had been feeding him liquid nourishment and medication over the last few months. His wife, Xena, was sitting next to him with their small child on her knee. The conclusion of Socrates's consultation with the doctors became immediately obvious when Xena started crying and saying that this was the last time he would be able to meet and talk with us. Socrates asked Chris—you must have met him, he was Socrates's oldest and most prosperous friend—if he could arrange for a doctor to give Xena something to help calm her down and an ambulance to take her home. Xena bid her husband and us farewell, crying hysterically.

"The nurse pushed Socrates's pillows back and helped him to recline. She rubbed the area where the tubes had fed into his veins. As she was rubbing, Socrates commented to us on the curious relationship between pleasure and pain. 'The two seem opposites. Yet they are closely connected with each other. People do not sense them both at once. But if you feel one of them, the other will follow, as sure as night follows day. Like Siamese twins, they are joined and cannot be separated. Wherever one comes, the other must follow. I imagine a fairy tale or fable about pain and pleasure of the sort that Aesop or the Grimm brothers might write and that Disney would make into a movie. Pain and pleasure would be represented as cartoon characters, like a cat and a mouse, or a dog and a cat, or some pair of animals that tend to quarrel with each other in cartoons. Then the king of the forest, or Brad Pitt or somebody like that, would decree that they stop quarreling, but when they defy the decree, Pitt would punish them by tying them together so they cannot go anywhere by themselves but must do everything together I am experiencing this curious phenomenon right now. The pain of the needles in my flesh is chased away by the pleasure of relief. The pain, in a sense, caused the pleasure.'

"Two of Socrates's students from Texas, Professors Sebastian and Simms, were with us. Sebastian interjected that it was good that Socrates mentioned Disney and the Grimm brothers because it reminded him of a question he wished to ask Socrates. He had heard back in Texas that Socrates spent some of his time in the hospice composing a romantic poem based on the Grimm brothers' 'Sleeping Beauty.' He had also heard that Socrates was composing a hymn of praise in ancient Greek.

"Everyone smiled at the thought of these wild rumors being true. Professor Sebastian continued, saying that before he came to New York, he had run into the poetic philosopher Euenus, who also wanted to know if Socrates had picked up poetry at the hospice after a lifetime of not writing a single line of verse.

"Socrates admitted that he had indeed been composing poems. But he asked Sebastian to let Euenus know that he need not worry about competition. 'I know it will not be easy to rival his poetry. I wrote "Sleeping Beauty" in verse because of my dreams. Well, you know how superstitious I am. . . . I had been having these dreams and I was not sure about their meaning, what they instructed me to do. So I have been suffering from a case of bad conscience. What if I should do what the dreams tell me? What if I misinterpret their meaning? All my life, I have had this recurring dream that had one message for me: Socrates, you must become an artist. I used to interpret it as telling me to do what I have been doing, practicing the art of being a philosopher, attempting to find out the truth by asking questions and critically discussing the answers I received. I used to interpret the dream as cheering me on to continue practicing the greatest art of all, philosophy, just as an audience cheers on its favorite athletes. But then I became chronically sick and had to move to this hospice. Now, you must have heard about people facing death changing in radical ways, wanting to put their house in order, deciding what is important to them. I also changed a little. I wanted to be sure that I did not misinterpret the instruction I received in my dream. So, to be on the safe side, I composed a poetic version of "Sleeping Beauty" in case the dream wanted me to be a poet. I also wrote some music for it, so I can claim to be a musician as well. Now, having obeyed the dream according to any interpretation, I can leave this world in good conscience. Earlier, I started with a few verses in a hymn for St. Cecilia because she is the patron saint of music. Once that was successful I decided to write something more serious with a story. Since I am not a storyteller but a debating philosopher, I decided to put into poetry an existing story. "Sleeping Beauty" was the first story that came to mind.'"

SUICIDE IS PAINLESS

"Socrates continued, 'This is what you should tell Euenus, Sebastian: Tell him good-bye for me. Tell him that if he is wise, he should follow me as soon as possible. As you know, I am leaving today.'

"'What advice!' proclaimed Professor Simms. 'Euenus and I

have been buddies for many years. I do not think he will follow your advice, unless he is forced to die. He loves life.'

"'But he is a philosopher as well as poet, is he not?' asked Socrates.

"'Of course he is,' affirmed Simms. 'So what?'

"'Well, anybody who is a philosopher or who at least has a philosophical perspective should not be afraid to die and should even die willingly. I do not mean that philosophers should take their own lives. Suicide is not right. But when death happens, it is welcomed.'

"The nurse straightened Socrates and sat him up in his bed, his withered and practically dead legs resting on the floor.

"Professor Sebastian then raised a very important question. 'If Socrates acknowledges that suicide is wrong and so philosophers should not take their own lives, why should they willingly follow those who die? Generally, many people think suicide is wrong. Most religions prohibit it. Many philosophers argue against it. But I have never quite understood their reasons.'

"'You should not be discouraged. If you persist, maybe one day, you will understand something. Just do not commit suicide in the meantime,' teased Socrates. He offered to rephrase the question in more general terms. 'Your question is, Why is accidental death sometimes a good thing, while planned death is always bad, yes? Generally, the death of a loved one like a spouse or a parent or a child is a bad thing. But there are some cases when it can be good, for example, if the loved one is in extreme and excruciating pain, or if their death happens before they would have committed some horrible crime or would have become wicked people. For example, if your beloved brother dies in a car accident on his way to murder somebody, his death is a good thing because he died an innocent man. Intuitively, it may seem that in some cases death is better than life. If it is better, at least for some people, to be dead than alive, why are they unable to solve their own problems and instead have to depend on somebody or something else? For example, if somebody's life is filled with pain or if it has lost any positive meaning, and that person dies in a car accident, we might say that they were lucky to have died when they did. But if instead of waiting for a car to run them over they take their own lives, we say it is bad. Why?'

"'Right on,' exclaimed Sebastian.

"Socrates acknowledged that there is an apparent internal inconsistency in the common objection to suicide. 'On the one hand, we accept that accidental death can sometimes be good, yet we think that suicide is always bad and can never be good. We accept that death is sometimes good when it is brought about by forces outside our control, but we never accept death as good when it is brought about by the person who benefits from their own death.

"'But maybe there is no inconsistency after all. We often hear rumors about what happens after death and what death is. Considering that soon I will find out for myself whether these rumors are true, I am curious to know what may await me.

"'The rumors we hear about a doctrine of life and death have a secret and unknown source. This doctrine holds that people are like prisoners who have no right to break the doors of their existence and escape the prison that is life. God is like the warden of the prison of life. God can decide our fate, if and when we are released from this life-prison. This rumored mystery resolves the incoherence of the common objection to suicide.

"'If we accept that humans belong to God just as cows or chickens belong to farmers, then we also have to accept that humans cannot have more freedom than domestic animals. God can punish us, just as we may punish a duck or a pig we own that decides to end its life and become roadkill before it is fat enough to be slaughtered and fetch the best price. If the relationship between God and humans is no different from that between a farmer and his pigs, then there can be no justification for suicide. On the contrary, there is every reason to argue that men and women must wait patiently and not take their own lives until God decides to intervene and create external circumstances when death becomes inevitable.'

"Professor Sebastian seemed impressed yet skeptical. He accepted Socrates's reasoning, but thought that his conclusions still seemed to contradict his claim that philosophers should be willing to die and should even accept death willingly. 'If you are right,' he told Socrates, 'God is our owner or warden or guard, and we are his property, pets, slaves, or cattle, it does not matter. We should be happy to be where we are, in the service of God. This may be our optimal situation in the world, having the best master and commander possible. Why would wise people like philosophers want to leave this service? Surely it is better to remain in the service of God than to be free. It would be sad to leave such a master, and a wise person would do all they could to avoid freedom. Only a truly stupid person would wish to escape such a splendid service, not realizing that it is much better to serve a good master than to be free. It seems then that rational and wise people try to avoid death and grieve when it happens, while only fools long to die and accept death willingly.'

"Socrates was delighted with Professor Sebastian's response. There was nothing better than a good criticism to develop an argument. He thanked Sebastian for his counterargument. He praised him as a true philosopher, one who does not accept arguments without subjecting them to critical analysis, investigating whether conclusions follow from arguments, and arguments follow from assumptions.

"Professor Simms seconded his colleague's objection to Socrates's claim. 'Sebastian is right. It does not seem plausible for a wise man to want to escape a master better than himself. It would be a thoughtless decision to wish to escape. When Professor Sebastian mentioned the foolish man who rushes thoughtlessly to escape a good master to gain worthless freedom in death, he may have been talking about you. When you are so excited, ready, and willing to leave us in death, you are also escaping the God who you acknowledged is a good master and ruler.'

"'Yes, I agree that you have presented me with a strong argument against the coherence of my argument. I would rather suffer anything than contradict myself or be inconsistent. I need to develop my argument, defend it so it can withstand the kind of effective criticisms you two have leveled against it.

"'Let me point out first that if life here in this world is guided by a divine master, I find no reason to believe that existence after death will be any different. So by dying, one is not escaping a wise master, if there is one, but rather is either sticking with the same master in a different place, or—if there is more than one god—perhaps replacing one master with another. If there is life after death in some sense, I may also meet much better people than those alive today. For this reason, I do not see any cause to grieve my own or anybody else's death.'

"Turning to Sebastian and Simms, Socrates said, 'I sincerely do not want to deprive you of the pleasure of grieving for me when I am gone, but for your argument to work, there must be a good god or gods in this world of the living and no continuous existence after death, or else that continued form of existence must be in a godless universe or in a world whose god is not as good as the one of this world. Only very few people would agree with that argument. Atheists do not think there is any god in any world. Most theists feel that the God they believe in during life also reigns in the afterlife.'

"Professor Simms pleaded with Socrates to share his opinions of what happens after death. Clearly, Socrates thought life continued in some altered state after death. Could he clarify his thoughts on the rarely explicitly discussed topic of what happens during and after death?

"As Socrates prepared to start a long speech, there was some commotion at the back of the room. Chris, Socrates's oldest friend, rushed to the back and returned with the news that one of the nurses had asked Socrates to stop debating because talking and arguing makes the body more resistant to medicinal intervention. Socrates laughed at the risible suggestion. He told Chris to tell the nurse to go to hell. He would talk until he dropped. If they needed to increase the dosage, so be it. Chris nodded; he had foreseen Socrates's reaction but had had to convey the nurse's request. He would make sure nobody disturbed us from then on.

"'Tell her to mind her own business. My business is philosophy,' exclaimed Socrates. 'You will be the judges of my claims. I argue that any true philosopher, who has lived his life philosophically, has no reason to grieve death. He accepts it cheerfully. After death, a philosopher can expect to have a better kind of existence than in this world. I will explain now how and why.'"

DEATH AS LIFE, LIFE AS DEATH

"'Simple people, who do not pursue wisdom as a way of life but who live a life of material production and consumption, often do not understand that philosophy is all about active preparation to die. Philosophers pursue death all their lives.

Therefore, when death finally arrives, it would be ridiculous to recoil in horror from something they have prepared for and pursued all their philosophical lives.'

"Professor Simms released a tense and nervous laugh when he heard Socrates's description of philosophy as the art of dying. 'I cannot help thinking of the response of uneducated people, like the managers who run my university, to what you say. This is no laughing matter. They will agree with you and use what you say to attack philosophy. They are already talking about abolishing the department. They will say that after studying your philosophy, they discover that philosophy desires life that is really death and teaches how to live in a way that is truly dying. They will then help us institutionally to die, close down our department and increase the budget of the medical school by a one-hundredth of a percent.'

"'They would be right, my dear Simms, except they really have no idea what is the essence of the death that philosophers desire and practice. As you noted, they are too ignorant of philosophy and unaccustomed to philosophical inquiry to be able to find out anything about it. Let us leave them alone to go on dumbing down the quality of higher education and emptying it of moral or intellectual content. Let us pursue our inquiry among friends in the usual dialogic method: do we believe that there is such a thing as death, or is it an illusion or a kind of linguistic confusion?'

"'Of course there is death,' affirmed Professor Simms.

"'If so, death must be the separation of something that persists after death, which we traditionally call "soul," from another part that is destroyed, which we traditionally call "body." Death is the separation of these two parts. The soul goes on existing by itself, unattached to the body. The body is left without a soul and then perishes and gradually disappears. Death is the release of the soul from the body. Correct?'

"'That is the traditional view, yes,' said Sebastian.

"'Let us move from death to the philosopher and add a few assumptions. Let me ask you: do you think philosophers, as philosophers, care or should care about the pleasures of eating and drinking? Would you consider philosophers generally to be gourmands?'

"Simms laughed. 'Maybe in France. But no, generally, I would say philosophers care little about what they eat or drink.'

"'Now, what about the pleasures of the flesh, erotic desires?'

"Simms laughed again. 'Good sex is not the first thing I would associate with philosophical activity. I had a colleague once who confused the two, but he was let go. Sexual harassment, you know.'

"'What about all the other ways we receive pleasure through the body and the senses, nice clothes, pretty shoes, glimmering jewels, fragrant perfumes, and so on? Do you think philosophers typically value such things or avoid them, unless they are necessary because even philosophers must eat some food and wear some clothes and walk in some shoes?'

"'I have never met a fashionable philosopher. We typically do not care how we are dressed and so on.'

"'Can we agree then that philosophers typically do not care much for their bodies, their needs and pleasures, but direct their attention away from the body and focus on the mind or soul; the terminology does not matter. Philosophers strive to free their minds from associations with the body and preoccupation with its pleasures and pains more than ordinary people and to the greatest extent possible because we can never be completely free of our bodies.'

"Sebastian and Simms agreed with this characterization of philosophers.

"'Ordinary people think that life devoid of physical pleasure is not worth living. If we cannot move and see and hear, most people would consider us dead, because they associate life with physical existence and pleasure derived from the senses, and death with the absence of a body.

"'Let us next consider becoming wise through acquiring knowledge. Does having a body help or hinder us in the search for wisdom? Are the senses such as sight and sound reliable guides to the truth, or are they constantly inaccurate? Our eyes show us things that are not there in optical illusions and fail to see things that are very small or very far away. When different people look at the same things, they sometimes see different things, for example, different colors. They cannot all be right. Likewise, there are auditory illusions that cause us to hear sounds that were not made. We cannot hear many things, for example, sounds that are beyond the range of our auditory organs that animals like dogs can hear. Also, people can hear different things when they listen to the same sound. Sight and sound are our better, senior, most reliable senses. Touch and smell are inferior to them. For example, whether we consider an object hot or cold depends on what we touched before. If you put your hand in a cold place like a freezer, the room will feel warm afterward. Vice versa, if you put your hand in hot water and then in luke-warm water, it will feel cold.

"'It seems, then, that the senses are deceiving and are even false witnesses. If our mind attempts to base its search for wisdom and truth on the senses, it is likely to err and be mis-guided. But as philosophers, we know of a better, more reliable method for obtaining the truth and gaining wisdom, by using our rational capacity to reason. But when our mind reasons and thinks, sights and sounds, pains and pleasures disrupt the reasoning. If there is a sound in the street below, or if the chil-dren turn on the television, or if the tooth starts to hurt, or if we begin to enjoy the company of our spouse, the result is distraction and disruption of the operation of reason. The best thing for the mind is to somehow disengage itself from the body and its distractions. When the soul is left alone, without being hampered by the body, without being bombarded by the senses with noises and sights and by the body with its pleasures and pains, the soul can finally achieve direct grasp of all that is. So the philosopher wishes to escape the body to protect the soul from bodily distractions and be able to perceive the truth itself, complete and unbiased by the unreliable imperfections of the senses.'

"'This is your concept of death, then,' mumbled Simms.

"But Socrates continued. 'As philosophers, we are not concerned exclusively with truth. We are also interested in the nature of justice, beauty, and goodness. We attempt to comprehend them in absolute universal terms. We are not interested in what is good or bad, just or unjust, beautiful or ugly, in a particular context at a particular time and place. We are interested in absolute justice, goodness, and beauty, what they are by themselves. Tell me, please, have you ever seen absolute beauty or justice or goodness with your eyes, or have you ever sensed them with any of the other senses?'

"'Of course not,' answered Simms. 'This world is full of beautiful, just, and good things that we can see or otherwise sense. But none of them is absolutely beautiful or just or good. Such absolute perfection is impossible.'

"'And the same thing holds for any absolute property we may want to understand and study, like absolute health, strength, and greatness. In other words, the true essence of everything is unattainable through the senses by observing the world around us. Perceiving essences, what is essentially beautiful or strong or just and so on, is achieved not through the senses but through reason, through our "mind's eye," through rational intuition. Only the pure mind can understand pure objects in their essences. Any interference from the senses, sight or sound, will only lead the pure mind astray, away from the knowledge of reality in its essence.

"'Philosophers love wisdom and seek the truth. While their souls are tied to their bodies and their thoughts mingle reason with sensory distractions, their quest for the truth is difficult, arduous, and, even after great efforts, unfulfilled. The body is a constant nuisance for philosophers. It makes us hungry, and so we must look for food. We need to spend time on working for food and then preparing and eating it. The body is susceptible to diseases. When we are sick, we may be overwhelmed by pain and incapable of clear thought. Our various emotions like desires for love and sex; fears, anxieties and phobias; the desire for all sorts of unimportant and unnecessary things; and the worshipping of idols in sports, television, and politics all crowd the poor mind and clutter it, leaving no space for contemplative thought.

"'Where do you think war and belligerence and partisanship come from, if not from the body and its desires and emotions? Greed causes war. People fight to steal land and homes and valuables and so on from other people. Where does this greed come from, if not from the base desires of the body to accumulate more and more things? Consequently, people lose colossal amounts of time on such wars and struggles. Only rarely does a philosopher emerge out of war. You know the legend about the philosopher René Descartes, who was also a mercenary? When he observed from atop the White Mountain in Prague the concluding battle of the Thirty Years' War in 1621 that was raging below him, he concluded that it is better to observe life than to participate in it.

"'By nature, our soul inclines to search for the truth. It has a propensity to live in truth. Given time and opportunity, it will move toward the truth. Humans are natural philosophers. The body just gets in the way. It confuses and interrupts our investigations, preventing us from allowing the truth to appear to us. You can think of the truth as a tune that is played constantly. We would all hear it if it were not for the constant background noise drowning it out. Every once in a while we notice the tune, but then the body immediately distracts us with some other loud and unpleasant noises. The only way to stop this "noise," for the soul to have the time and peace of mind to hear the truth, is by silencing the body. Only then can philosophers fulfill their love of wisdom and attain the truth. This cannot happen while we live, but it may be achieved after we are dead, when the soul is finally released from the body. In this life, we get nearest to the truth, to knowledge when we are least concerned about our bodies and their interests. We strive to contain the influences of the body on our mind and wait patiently until God finally releases us from our bodies. Then and only then can our souls be pure, come into contact and communicate with other such pure souls, and together attain the pure truth, the absolute essences of things. This is the inevitable conclusion of accepting the philosophical life, which is a kind of death. Philosophy is about separating the soul from the body, concentrating it far away from the senses and emotions, and finally releasing it from the sickbed of life and the feeding tubes of material nourishment. A true philosopher constantly attempts to separate soul from body, to achieve freedom. Ultimate freedom, then, is death. Would it not be ridiculous if somebody who spends their whole life attempting to approach a state of separation of their soul from their bodies—a state that resembles death—recoiled in horror when that release of the soul was about to be finally achieved in death?!

"'For this reason, philosophers are more ready to die than anybody else. They know there is nothing to be afraid of; on the contrary, there is much to expect. Their existence is closer to death than anybody's among the living. After all, they have always been the enemies of the body. In death, philosophers get the chance to attain the true knowledge and wisdom they have pined for, to finally rid themselves of the body and break the shackles that tie them to material reality.

"'Compare this view of death, the separation of soul from body and its direct interaction with the eternal truths, with the common, vulgar view of life after death: Some people believe that after death they will meet again with loved ones they lost, like parents and spouses. In general, many people seem to believe that life after death will be very much like life here, only a bit better. They believe that we will live in bigger houses with our spouses at our best physical age. They believe that after death we will see and hear and smell just as we do in life.'

"'It is Hollywood that spreads this nonsense,' interjected Chris. 'It is impossible to visually present a form of existence that is not material. When the body dies, the five external senses die with it. There will be no visions or sounds or smells or touch after death. So how can it be represented to nonphilosophers with limited rational imagination? Choirs of angels with harps?'

"We all laughed as Chris continued to denounce the vulgar concept of existence after death. 'Where does this concept of living in a perfect garden after death come from? Where does the idea of a burning-hot hell come from? When the body is dead, there is no garden to see or touch and no skin to sense heat. The concepts of heaven and hell originated among cultures in arid climates where heat was a problem and luscious gardens were scarce. Had the Eskimos written our myths, hell would have been frozen and heaven would be a sunny beach. Some religions even suggest that there is sex after death in that garden. Do dead souls make babies?'

"We laughed again, and Socrates resumed his speech in favor of a philosophical approach to death. 'If we expect that what we really want will be realized after death, we have nothing to be afraid of and no need to worry about death. In the legend of Orpheus and Eurydice, Orpheus follows his love willingly to the underworld after she dies, just as the philosopher, the lover of wisdom, follows his or her love, wisdom, beyond death. The prospect of coming into direct contact with the truth and wisdom after death should fill the philosopher with expectant joy, just as the prospect of reuniting with his wife would have filled Orpheus with joy. Pure wisdom can be achieved only through death. Therefore, there is nothing to fear about death.'

"Chris nodded in agreement. 'Fear of death is an indication of ignorance of what death is, and it is then fear of the unknown. When people who claim to believe in some kind of life after death display fear of death, it indicates that they do not believe in what they proclaim. Had they believed they were going to a better world, they would not have feared death or attempted desperately to avoid it.'

"'Or they may not be lovers of wisdom,' suggested Socrates. 'People who are excessively attached to their bodies or to money or to power have every reason to attempt to avoid death. In death, they will gain the possibility of acquiring pure wisdom, but they will have to leave behind all the things they acquired and valued in this life.'

"Simms nodded his agreement. 'This is absolutely true, Socrates.'

"'Let us then consider the special virtues of being a philosopher, the kind of virtues that true philosophers usually possess,' Socrates continued. "Courage must be one. Self-control and prudence must be others. These virtues are marked by their disdain of and control over passions, fears, and desires. Such disregard of bodily passions is typical of the true philosopher. Only philosophers can be truly courageous and in control of their emotions. If nonphilosophers seem to be courageous and in control of their bodily desires, this is only an appearance based on its diametrical opposite.'

"Simms was bewildered by this statement. He asked Socrates to explain how an apparent virtue can be based on its opposite vice.

"'It is very simple,' explained Socrates. 'Fear is the opposite vice to courage. Now, when somebody who is not a philosopher appears to show courage facing death, it can be the result of the opposite of courage, fear of something that person considers more frightening than death, like physical or mental pain. The person who appears courageous is actually a coward. Philosophical courage when facing death is not founded on fear of something worse but on disdain for the body and acceptance of death as a way to get rid of it in pursuit of truth and wisdom.

"'The same can be said of self-control. What appears to be virtuous self-control may actually be the result of the opposite vice of calculating desire. For example, somebody may control their desire to kill somebody not as a manifestation of virtuous self-control but from the vice of calculating self-interest, fearing incarceration and preferring to satisfy the murderous hatred some other time, in stealth, without being punished. Similarly, nonphilosophers who appear to be controlling their desires are actually enslaved to other, stronger desires. Only true philosophers control all their desires for the sake of controlling them rather than for satisfying more of them at the expense of others. The overwhelming consideration is that of maximizing pleasure, not acting virtuously. Similarly, the coward I mentioned earlier, who preferred death to something else that he was more afraid of, made a computation that in the end was motivated by fear. We can generalize then that when nonphilosophers appear to display philosophical virtues, it is usually the result of deeper vices whose satisfaction is maximized in this way. The underlying value of all these maximizing computations is physical pleasure.

"'But there is a much better universal currency for measuring the values of our actions, and that is wisdom. Courage, self-control, and justice can buy us wisdom. With wisdom we can also buy self-control, courage, and justice. The virtues receive their value from their exchange value with wisdom. "Virtues" that cannot be exchanged for wisdom but only for one another, pleasure for pleasure, lack of fear for lack of fear, and so on, are false virtues.

"'Wisdom is a kind of purification of the soul from the contamination of pleasures and fears that allows the truth to be perceived. Many different mystical cults and religions instructed their believers to go through purification rituals like baptism to prepare themselves for death. If we interpret such rituals metaphorically, there is a kernel of truth in them. We do need to "purify" ourselves to prepare for death. But this "purification" is not about cleaning our bodies with water or anything else. The purification is a symbol for wisdom ridding us of the emotions and desires that contaminate our soul. Philosophers who go through this kind of purification of their souls through wisdom are ready to die. I have spent my whole life preparing to die. I have attempted to use my wisdom to purify my soul of my body, not sparing any opportunity to advance the cause of wisdom.

"'My dear Sebastian and Simms, this is all the defense I have of my view of life and death and of why a philosopher should welcome death happily but not seek to commit suicide.

At the very least, you understand now why I am ready to leave life behind without grieving, without resistance, and without resentment. I believe it will be better for me on the other side.'"

BODY AND SOUL

"Professor Simms, who listened intently to Socrates's long speech in defense of his joyful acceptance of death as a route to wisdom and truth, stepped forward to interrupt the discussion. 'I agree with much of what you have to say about philosophical virtue and life devoted to wisdom rather than pleasure. But I have serious doubts about your account of the soul. Many people think that death is not just of the body, as you put it, but also of what you call the soul. The mind, our consciousness, may die together with the body. Perhaps it is inevitable that the mind dies with the body because it cannot exist independently of it. You may dislike the unfortunate association of mind with body, of mind with brain, for example, but it may be necessary. Consciousness will vanish when the body is destroyed, as fire is quenched when all the wood is burned. What awaits us after death, then, is nothing, not wisdom or truth, not pain or suffering, just nothing. What you say about our approach to death makes sense only if there is a soul that can exist independently of the body and that can then be released from this unfortunate association with death. You need to prove, and you have not so far, that the soul continues to exist after death and that it has some properties that allow it to enjoy wisdom and truth. The soul must retain its intelligence and have some force of self-direction and self-movement, even without a physical existence. It needs to be able to direct itself to the truth in the nonphysical universe it would exist in.'

"'You have raised a number of important points that I would like to address,' acknowledged Socrates gravely.

"'Take all the time you need,' replied Professor Sebastian. 'I really want to know your opinion about these issues.'

"Socrates prepared himself for another speech in defense of his views on the immortality and preservation of the soul. 'You remember that satirical playwright who made fun of me and philosophy some years ago in his play *Skyscrapers*? He made me look literally like a lunatic, climbing up skyscrapers to get closer to the truth and away from the noise and multitudes below. The play attempted to make fun of philosophers as people detached from reality in search of reality. Well, now nobody, not even that playwright, could ridicule me for discussing silly topics that are none of my business. I proceed in my inquiry about what will or will not happen to me in a few hours.

"'I have been advocating a version of the ancient doctrine of reincarnation of souls that can be traced back at least to the ancient Hindu faith in India. Generally speaking, the reincarnation doctrine claims that after death, souls transmigrate to a different kind of universe that is not material or physical. Then, later, they return to our world from that world and are born again into a new body. In this sense, life is generated from death. If souls are reincarnated, and the living come from the dead, then the souls must go to and then come from somewhere in between, a nonphysical world into which they migrate after death. So my argument will rely on attempting to prove that the living are born of the dead. If I can prove that, it follows that death is the separation of the destroyed body from the soul that migrates to another world and from there back to this one to be reborn.'

"Professor Sebastian agreed. 'If the living are born from the souls of the dead, then there is a strong argument in favor of the preservation of the soul beyond death. But can you prove reincarnation?'"

THERE IS A BALANCE IN THE FORCE

"'I think it will be easier for me to prove reincarnation if we consider life in general—not just human life but also animal and plant life. Common to all forms of life is that they become what they are in the process of generation. Take any form of life: there was a time when it was not here and it had to be generated. Every life will also perish.

"'I want to introduce here a general thesis about generation. Everything that is generated, is generated from its opposite. To give an obvious example, for anything to become bigger or longer, it must have been smaller or shorter first. The less must have been first more, and the more, less. The same holds true for the faster and slower, stronger and weaker, worse and better, and so on.

"'Opposites generate each other through processes that constantly follow each other to and fro, forward and backward; for example, through growth and decay, and waxing and waning. Other processes are of cooling and heating, contracting and expanding, and so on.'

"Professor Simms considered Socrates's theory and asked, 'If my little daughter grows by one inch over a month, would you say that she became taller from its opposite, shorter? If I lose one pound from my weight, would you say that thin was generated from fat?'

"'Absolutely, yes,' replied Socrates. 'So, for our topic, we need to look for the opposite of life from which it must be generated, as sleep is the opposite of being awake.'

"'You obviously mean death,' replied Sebastian.

"'Of course! Death is generated from life, and life is generated from death; one opposite generates the other. Everybody knows that life generates death. The crucial point of my argument is to prove that death also generates life. Most important to me is that by "death," I mean souls existing in another, nonphysical, world.

"'I do not need to prove that life generates death because that is visibly apparent. The act of dying, in which I am about to indulge myself, can be observed by anybody. But I would go so far as to infer from this observable process its complementary opposite process from death to life, which is invisible. If we recognize a universal law of opposites that generate each other symmetrically, the generation of life from death must be symmetrical to that of the generation of death from life.'

"'You mean resurrection of the dead in the world of the living?' asked Sebastian.

"'Yes, precisely. If we recognize a universal law of opposites generating each other, there must be a symmetrical, complementary process to that of the generation of death from life. If the dead generate life, they must come from somewhere, and that "place" must be a nonphysical universe where they dwell after one life and before another. Have I not proved my point?'

"Professor Sebastian pondered the matter and answered, 'If you assume that death means the existence of souls in a nonphysical universe, and if you assume that opposites must generate each other, it certainly follows that souls must exist in a nonphysical universe and generate life. But I can imagine some philosophers might take issue with your assumption of the meaning of death.'

"'Look at it in another way,' suggested Socrates. 'Suppose that opposites were not generating each other in an eternal cyclical process like in economic booms and busts, or sleep and wakefulness—what kind of world would we be living in? It would be a world with little or no change. Once one opposite generates an opposite, it would just remain in that state. Once we fall asleep, we would remain asleep forever, like Sleeping Beauty in my poem. Once we awaken, we would remain awake forever. Once the hot becomes cold, it remains so, and vice versa, when the cold generates the hot, it would remain hot, and so on. We would be living, then, in a world where everything is static, with no change. Since we obviously live in a world full of change, there must be cyclical generation of opposite from opposite.

"'Let us apply this general observation to the life and death issues that concern us here: If living things died without generating life, gradually and eventually, all life would become extinct and would die. If at the same time dead things did not become alive again, life would disappear.'

"'Unless life comes from other forms of life,' interjected Professor Simms. 'If there is a direct genealogical line between us and the first unicellular forms of lives that may have been generated from inanimate matter, life generates life. The process of life can move in a straight line rather than being cyclical, as you put it.'

"'Oh, stop interjecting modern science into ancient philosophy,' reprimanded Socrates. 'I heard you whispering before your criticism of my analysis of the ultimate constituents of the world as made of opposites. You suggested instead that the world can be made of degrees of the same things. So, cold and hot are no longer opposites but different degrees of the same thing that modern physics calls kinetic energy. But if you want to have a dialogue with me, you have to respect your ancients, and I am very ancient indeed.

"'My own firm belief is that life must come from death, and that therefore the souls of the departed must exist in a non-physical universe of their own.'"

REMEMBRANCE OF LOST TIME

"Sebastian looked at Socrates sympathetically. 'Perhaps I can offer another, different argument for the theory of souls and their reincarnation that you presented. You recall your theory of knowledge, of what is knowledge and where it comes from? You have been arguing that learning is remembering. If everything we truly know, in contrast to the opinions we have about things, is remembered rather than acquired in the present, there must have been some time when those memories were acquired. Since we are born with this knowledge, there must have been a time before birth when this knowledge could have been acquired. Since we did not have a body prior to birth, we must have had some kind of nonphysical existence, so our souls were able to acquire this knowledge through some other way than the senses.'

"Professor Simms asked his colleague Sebastian to present and support this theory of learning as remembering, of knowledge as recollection. 'I must have missed the discussion where Socrates introduced this theory,' he explained, 'or perhaps I just do not remember the discussion just now.'

"Professor Sebastian proceeded to explain. 'One proof is from the form of our dialogues with Socrates. Socrates's method has become so famous that it is named after him: the Socratic method. Socrates asks us general questions about the nature of concepts like justice, or being cool, or piety. We answer him, and then he questions our answers. Where does our knowledge of the concepts come from? Nobody has ever taught us what justice is in general. Some years ago, Socrates "taught" a formally uneducated person, a chauffeur, the basic rules of logic without telling him what they were; he just reminded him of what he already knew and allowed him to rediscover that knowledge himself. When Socrates was a high school teacher, he taught geometry in this way. He never dictated geometric deductions but rather allowed the students to discover them for themselves, by asking them the right questions, by "reminding" them. One explanation of what we remember when we answer the types of abstract questions Socrates asks may be that we remember our existence before we were born, when we lived a nonphysical, spiritual kind of existence and interacted directly with abstract objects like justice and the like.'

"Socrates intervened then to ask Simms if he was convinced by Sebastian's summary of his argument or if he required further proof. Simms answered that it was not a matter of being convinced. If Socrates's 'remembering' theory of knowledge was right, he ought to remember the correct answer rather than need to be convinced of it. Simms felt like he began to remember, but he needed to be reminded some more. So Socrates obliged him. 'Would you agree with me that to remember, a person must have known something previously?'

"'Of course, that is obvious,' affirmed Simms.

"'So let us briefly consider the nature of memory. How do we come to remember things? When we have some sensual stimulation, like when we see something or hear something, we gain some knowledge of it. But we also often gain another kind of knowledge that is distinct from yet associated with the first. When we move from the first kind of knowledge to the second, we say that we have been reminded of it.'

"Simms seemed a little bewildered, so Socrates proceeded to offer a few examples: 'When people are in love, if they perceive something that they associate with the object of their affection, they are reminded of her or him. They may hear a song they heard once in the company of their lover, or taste a dish they once ate in the company of their lover, or feel a fabric their lover once wore, and at once know both the sense object—the song, the taste of the dish, or the texture of the fabric—as well as something entirely different: the love relationship. We move from the first kind of knowledge to the second kind through being reminded. To take an obvious personal example, since you two, Simms and Sebastian, were my students at the same time and you always came and went together, whenever I see one of you, I am always reminded of the other.'

"'Indeed, these kinds of associations are the most common way we are reminded of things we remember,' said Simms. 'For example, when I need to remember PIN codes, I create an association with an important date in history or the birthday of a loved one, so knowing one will help me by association to remember the PIN code. If, for example, I need to recall the number 1215, I associate it with the date the Magna Carta was signed.'

"'That's right,' said Socrates. 'Would you agree that the association that leads to reminding does not have to be between similar objects that are alike in some respect? It can be between two things that have nothing in common.'

"'Of course,' agreed Simms. 'Associations are often idiosyncratic, as in poetry, psychoanalysis, and, indeed, memory.'

"'Now let us consider a different issue: equality or identity. Look at these two cups of water.' Socrates nodded toward the two cups of water on his bedside table. 'Are they equal to each other? Or, compare the chairs you sit on. Are they equal to each other?'

"'They are very similar,' replied Simms. 'But they are not absolutely identical or equal. The two cups hold very similar quantities of water, but if we subject them to laboratory tests, we will discover that the quantities of water in each cup are not identical. The two chairs have an identical design. But they are not equal. The texture of the wood is similar but not identical. The paint, too, is similar but not identical. They have different scratches and stains and so on, so they are not absolutely equal, though they are very similar.'

"'Very true, Simms. In ordinary language we say about such things that they are equal or the same or identical, but we never mean absolute identity. We can generalize this conclusion to all objects: many things resemble or are similar to each other, but no material object can ever be absolutely equal to another.'

"Simms concurred.

"'We agree that there is no absolute equality in the world. The approximate equalities between the cups of water and the chairs reminded us of absolute equality, but they fell short of it. Yet the relationships between these two cups of water and these two chairs somehow remind us of absolute equality. We cannot remember any absolute equality that we observed in this world in the past because there is none. So where did we gain knowledge of absolute equality?'

"'What is the relationship then between the kind of things we call equal in everyday contexts and absolute equality?' inquired Simms.

"'What does it matter?' Socrates shrugged off the question. 'We agreed earlier that when things are associated in our minds, both similar and dissimilar things can remind us of one another. It is important that the relationship between the two cups of water somehow reminded us of absolute equality.'

"'But surely absolute equality and imperfect equalities that we observe in everyday life are related somehow?' asked Simms.

"'That relationship must be of approximation,' replied Socrates. 'We can observe many things and judge that they are attempts to approximate or imitate something else, sometimes quite poorly. For example, you can see teenage boys everywhere trying to imitate an idol like Justin Bieber by dressing like him and having the same haircut as him. Some rock bands try to imitate more successful ones. Manufacturers generate cheap imitations of brand-name watches, bags, and clothing, but these cheap knockoffs are made of shoddy materials with inferior craftsmanship. How can we distinguish an imitation, a bad approximation of the real thing? For example, how can we tell that this young hospital orderly here with the gel in his hair and the tight jeans is a phony and not the real Justin Bieber?'

"'We compare the original that we remember with the imitation. This is not Justin Bieber. Rip-offs of Rolex® watches and Gucci® bags do not compare favorably with the originals. If we had never seen a real Rolex or a Gucci bag or at least a picture of them somewhere, we would not be able to judge their imitations as phony.'

"'That's right,' agreed Socrates. 'Now let us apply this insight to the case of equality between chairs and cups of water that we have been considering. We agreed that the quantity of water in these two cups is not absolutely equal and that the two chairs are not absolutely identical. How can we know? Unless—'

"'Unless we are already directly acquainted with absolute equality and identity and then compare the imperfect approximations we observe to the original we already know.' Simms completed Socrates's sentence.

"'Dear Simms, you were right before you were born, and so was I. But note one more difference between absolute equality and its approximation: when we measure the relationships between things in the world, whether they approximate equality or not, we use our senses: sight, touch, even hearing if we compare sounds, but to comprehend absolute equality, we do not use any of these senses. If we cannot learn about absolute equality from any of our sense experiences, how do we come to know it?

"'My conclusion, yet again, is that this knowledge must have been learned before we were born. We existed as souls prior to this life and will continue to exist as souls after this life. We acquired all the absolute ideas that we use to measure things before we were born. By this I mean all the ideas that value and evaluate, like equality, beauty, goodness, justice, holiness, and so on. Think of beauty, for example. We evaluate many things as very beautiful: the Parthenon in Athens, Beethoven's Ninth Symphony, da Vinci's *Mona Lisa*, Angelina Jolie—and maybe Brad Pitt as well. But as beautiful as they may be, none is absolutely beautiful. In fact, there is nothing absolutely beautiful on this earth. Yet we are able to evaluate how beautiful things are by comparing them with some ideal absolute beauty. The ideal of absolute beauty operates like a ruler or thermometer that measures less beautiful things. Since there is nothing absolutely beautiful in the material world, and since we obviously possess and use this idea, we must have acquired it somewhere. Again, this evidence points toward a prenatal source, when the soul could come into contact with and acquire pure ideas.

"'The same holds for all the concepts I have been inquiring about in the last half century, from justice to piety to being cool. They are all absolute and have no instantiation in this world. Our knowledge of these concepts does not come through the senses. We acquire it prior to our birth. I have been doing in my philosophical life nothing other than reminding myself and others of these absolute concepts.

"'Since we do not learn of absolute ideas like justice or length or equality from sense experiences, either we are born with all this knowledge or we learn it through recollection of things that we knew before we were born but that we have forgotten.

"'You look bewildered, Simms. What do you think? Do we possess all knowledge since birth and retain it, or do we need to remember things we knew in our previous lives as souls before our birth, as I have been suggesting?'

"It was not clear to me if Professor Simms's apparent bewilderment was real or a pose he learned from Socrates, appearing to be ignorant to expose the weaknesses in his interlocutor's views.

"Simms said, 'I really do not know. On the one hand, your theory of ideas is very fancy. It requires us to believe in an additional universe to the one we know and live in. It requires us to believe in the separate and eternal existence of souls. Finally, we also need to believe in a complicated process of learning in that parallel spiritual universe, forgetting, and then remembering as learning in this universe. You tell us very little about souls and how they acquire, retain, forget, and then recollect information. By contrast, if we believe that we are born with conceptual knowledge, as philosophers called rationalists do, we need to assume just one fancy theory, namely, that we are born with this stuff in our heads. That is two fewer fancy assumptions: no need for another universe, and no need for fancy entities like souls. We would still need to explain why we are born with conceptual knowledge, but there are convincing stories about how the process of biological evolution selected the kind of innate conceptual knowledge that is most conducive to survival. Such selection ensures that the way we conceptualize the world is true not in some ultimate sense but in a pragmatic sense of having a useful conceptualization of the world that favors survival and reproduction. Our conceptual knowledge may also be a by-product of the architecture of the brain. These two stories may be combined into one. There are other philosophers who make no assumptions about either being born with knowledge or remembering it from the time before we were born; they just try to describe how we can infer concepts from sense experiences. These philosophers are known as empiricists—'

"'Stop right there,' interrupted Socrates. 'Recall what I told you earlier! I am an ancient philosopher and please respect that. If every human being is in possession of knowledge from birth, why do we need to discuss these issues in the first place? Would we not already know all the answers we have been looking for regarding the nature of knowledge: what is life; are there souls, and if so, are they immortal; and so on?'

"Simms shook his head in disapproval. 'Clearly this is not such a world. Some people are more philosophical than others. I fear that in a few hours, there will be nobody left who is qualified to explain or even discuss these issues, once you are not with us anymore.'

"'If we agree that people are not equally knowledgeable and clever about these issues, how can you explain that? I suggest the difference is that some people remember better what they learned before they were born than others. Some have better associations and better stimulations to start the process of association and remembering. Attempting to answer the kinds of questions that I pose is very effective in eliciting conceptual memories. But maybe some souls also had better learning experiences before they were born. My point is that we must assume there was life before birth to explain different levels of conceptual knowledge.'

"Sebastian objected then. 'But there is yet another possibility. What if we acquire all the knowledge at the very moment of being born? We take our first breath, and then somehow, we gain all the knowledge. Some of us may be better at gaining it or may somehow receive more knowledge than others. In this way, we do not have to assume eternal souls and life before birth.'

"Simms looked at Sebastian, nodded in approval, and then added his own criticism. 'All human beings speak a mother tongue. We learn it after we are born; that is why people speak different languages. If Noam Chomsky is right, we are all born with a universal grammar that fits all languages; it is in the architecture of our brains. We do not need to live before birth to acquire it. More significantly, most people do not know the formal rules of grammar of their mother tongue, and almost nobody knows the formal rules of universal grammar that Chomsky introduced. They know them tacitly but not explicitly. You need to distinguish the kind of tacit knowledge that everybody might have once their brains reach a certain level of development from the kind of explicit, reflective knowledge we are discussing here.'

"'Well, there you go again, Simms. If you introduce one more modern thought to this discussion, I will expel you from this dialogue for good. Who is this Chomsky, anyway—some anarchist?! Let me address the much older and more respectable concerns that Sebastian raised. If learning is remembering, as we agreed, there has to be an act of forgetting first. If we did not forget what we knew, there would be nothing to remember later. We need to ask when the forgetting happens. If we acquire knowledge before birth, we forget it when we are born. That is simple. But if we acquire knowledge at birth, when should we forget it? Immediately after we gain it?'

"Simms wiped his brow and declared, 'You are absolutely right, Socrates. I was talking modern nonsense. It is much more plausible that souls without bodies acquire knowledge in a parallel universe and then forget that knowledge when they are born again in fresh bodies.'"

THE THEORY OF IDEAS

"Socrates was satisfied with Simms's response. 'There is one last philosophical repercussion of our discussion that I need to stress now: its effect on ontology. Ontology is the study of what is, or of being. Our ontology is broader than the one people admit to in everyday life. It includes souls that can exist without bodies in a nonphysical universe. In such a universe, they can come into direct contact with absolute abstract ideas that also exist by themselves without any physical instantiation. Absolute ideas like beauty and justice, equality and piety, but also less abstract ideas like cookie and chair exist there without being attached to objects. As much as souls can exist without a body, beauty can exist without being attached as a property to any object. Justice can exist by itself without regulating the interactions between people. The idea of a cookie can exist by itself without being attached to any dough, and so on. Physical objects that exemplify these ideas are pale reflections, imitations of their ideas. All the chairs in the world are imitations of the ideal chair. All the beautiful people in the world are pale reflections of beauty itself. Our prior acquaintance with ideas like beauty, justice, or chair allow us to measure which physical objects are more or less beautiful and which chairs are more perfect chairs than others.

"'The relationships between the absolute and perfect ideas and their reflections or imitations in the real world lead us to call them essences. The essence of this chair here is the ideal chair. It has no color or prescribed shape or material because the ideal of the chair is not made of wood or metal and does not have any particular color or shape. Likewise, the idea of beauty is the essence of beautiful things like Beethoven's symphonies and Miró's paintings, though there are many things in the symphonies and paintings that are neither beautiful nor ugly. The essence of just acts is the idea of justice. Being fallible and human, any attempt to be just will always fall short of this idea. The same holds true for goodness and equality and so on.'

"Socrates looked at Sebastian with discontent. 'What? Have I browbeaten you into silence? You are still unconvinced?'"

SOULS AND THEIR MATES

"'Leave him alone, he is convinced.' Simms rushed to defend his best friend. 'Sebastian is stubborn and skeptical, but I think by now he believes in the existence of the soul before birth. However, you have not yet proved that the soul also exists after death. To be honest, although I am more on your side, I cannot say that I am convinced of it either. I—and Sebastian, too, I think—and many other people believe that the soul may simply disappear together with the body. Perhaps the soul cannot exist separately of the body. When the body dies, the soul, the mind, consciousness, whatever you care to call it, disintegrates with it, melts away, like tears in the rain. The emotions and behavior of many people also indicate that they do not believe they will live in some form after death.

"'Even if you manage to convince us that the soul must exist before birth, where it acquires the knowledge that we remember later, it does not follow that the soul continues to exist after death. The soul may be generated long before birth, then be united with the body and come to an end with it.'

"Emboldened by his friend's argument, Sebastian rejoined the discussion. 'Very true, dear friend. If the souls are eternal, they must exist both before birth and after death. So far, everything Socrates has said concerned life *before* birth. He said nothing and proved even less about life after death. Somehow, I think most people are more interested in living after they die than in learning that they had lived before they were born. Unfortunately, Socrates has not provided us with a proof for the soul's existence after death.'

"'But I have,' protested Socrates. 'You just need to put together the two proofs I have already presented. First, the argument from opposites: that one opposite always generates

196 PLATO FOR EVERYONE

another, and so life must come from death, just as death comes from life. Second, the argument from the existence of knowledge as remembrance of what the soul learned before it was born. If you put these two arguments together, you find that life results from the rebirth of souls that existed before in communion with the abstract ideas that they can remember.

"'Still, I suspect that you and Simms have an ulterior motive for examining my argument in such great detail. You are afraid. Like little children, you are afraid of death. Booo! Scary! What are you afraid may happen to you? Boring heaven or scorching hell? If nothingness, then there is nothing to be afraid of. If, as Monty Python quipped, you come from nothing and you are going back into nothing, what have you lost? Nothing! You are afraid of nothing. Isn't this silly?'

"Professor Sebastian smiled at Socrates's ridicule of the fear of death. 'If we are scared and you think we should not be, you must argue to prove that we have nothing to be afraid of. These fears are not ours in the strict sense of "our." There is a child in us all. That child is afraid of death. We have to imagine our adult selves sitting alone in the dark with our child-self who is trembling thinking of death. We have to calm down that child who is afraid of ghosts, zombies, and banshees, all personifications of our childish fears of death in different cultures.'

"'Perhaps you should sing him a philosophical lullaby every night, until the child calms down and is ready to go to sleep,' suggested Socrates. 'You can use the poem I composed based on "Sleeping Beauty."'

"Sebastian spoke for all of us when he asked, 'But who will make up and sing us such philosophical lullabies when you are gone, Socrates?'

"'The world is a big place, and there are many good people in it; people of all kinds and from different places. When I am dead, you should look for such people everywhere and spare neither time, nor effort, nor expense in that search, for there is no better reason to spend money.'

"'We will certainly conduct such a search,' reassured Sebastian and Simms. 'But let us return to the philosophical discussion of the soul at the point when we digressed to mention the emotional and psychological reactions many people have to death.'"

BACK TO THE IDEAS

"'By all means,' agreed Socrates. 'Let us consider the soul. In discussing its possible mortality or immortality, we need to consider first which kinds of things come into being and then disappear and which kinds of things remain unchanged forever. Let me make a suggestion: Compounds, things that are composed of different elements, are unstable; the bonds that keep them together may weaken, and they may fall apart and disappear. By contrast, homogenous, united entities cannot be dissolved. For example, it is much easier to carry by hand one large watermelon than many small lemons because the lemons will fall out of your hand. It is easier to keep together a country that is homogenous than a country that is made up of different linguistic, cultural, and religious groups. Multinational empires disintegrate more quickly than nation-states. A machine or instrument or piece of furniture is more stable if it is made of fewer parts, and so on.'

"'You are right on the whole, but some chemical elements, especially heavy ones of high atomic number, are more unstable than many chemical compounds,' said Sebastian.

"'Yes,' acknowledged Socrates. 'But that is because they are compounds of neutrons, positrons, electrons, and so on; and positrons and neutrons are themselves compounds of quantum particles. You remember Professor Piers Menides's riddle?'

"'Sure.' Sebastian smiled in nostalgic appreciation, as did the rest of us. When we were college students, we spent many happy hours trying to pick it apart and solve or dissolve it.

"Sebastian explained, 'If we agree that being exists and that nothingness does not exist, then being must be completely unified, because it would not be divided by nothing, which does not exist. What exists must also be everywhere the same, because there is no nothing to dilute it. Being must also be infinite in space and time because the only thing that could limit it is nothingness, and we assumed that nothingness does not exist. Being also cannot change, because it cannot change into nothingness, which we agreed does not exist. We start with two indisputable assumptions and reach the conclusion that the heterogeneous, diverse, and limited world we observe is impossible.' Sebastian laughed. 'We spent years trying to pick apart that one to avoid the absurd conclusion.'

"'That's right.' Socrates praised Sebastian's excellent memory. 'I think old Professor Piers Menides was basically right. True, the world we observe is different from his unified limitless Being because it is made of compounds of different types of things that exist. But things that are uncompounded share their properties with his Being; they do not change and always remain the same.

"'Now let us apply this insight to what we were discussing earlier. We talked of the essences of things, ideas that exist in their conceptual purity and perfection, separately from the poor imitations that we observe around us, ideas like beauty or goodness. Would we describe an idea like beauty as composite and changing or as always remaining the same and never changing? Think of the idea of equality that we discussed earlier. Does the idea of equality depend on its context? Does equality differ from place to place or culture to culture; does it change from time to time, or is equality just equal anywhere?'

"Sebastian affirmed that ideal essences do not seem to change at all, not according to their contexts and not in time.

"Socrates continued comparing the changing world we live in to the unchanging essences of things, the ideas. 'Now, consider not the ideas themselves but their reflections or imitations, whatever we want to call the things we see around us. Consider beautiful things, for example. There are beautiful people, beautiful paintings, beautiful clothes, and so on. Are all these beautiful things the same, or are they different, constantly changing with fashions and tastes?'

"'Historically, tastes and fashions change, of course. What people considered beautiful art and clothing two centuries ago is out of fashion today. What some people consider beautiful music, others consider worthless noise.'

"'You've got it,' exclaimed Socrates, praising Sebastian. 'Now let us think about epistemology, the theory of knowledge. How do we know about these two types of things, the ideas and their reflections? For example, how do we know about the idea of beauty, and how do we know if this poster of scenery in Switzerland and these plastic flowers in front of me are beautiful? Well, we can see if this poster is beautiful or not. Likewise, we use our sense of sight to observe how beautiful things like plastic flowers are. We use our sense of hearing to spot a beautiful tune. We use our sense of smell to decide which perfume smells nice, and our sense of taste to decide which dish has a delicate taste. But to understand what the idea of beauty is— the essence of all those various manifestations of beauty—the senses are of no use at all. We have to use a sixth sense to understand any of the ideas or essences of things. That sense is in the mind itself. It is sometimes referred to metaphorically as the "mind's eye." Rational intuition in our mind allows us to comprehend unchanging ideas that exist outside of the space and time where we happen to dwell. The mind allows us to perceive independently of the senses abstract and pure ideas like equality or justice or beauty that cannot be perceived through the senses.'

"Sebastian offered to sum up Socrates's theory of ideas or essences, asking him to correct him if he got anything wrong. 'To put it simply, you divide everything into two classes: material objects we can perceive through our senses, and abstract ideas we cannot perceive through those senses but can comprehend through our minds. The ideas we perceive through the mind and not the senses always remain the same in all contexts; they never change. By contrast, the material objects we perceive through the senses change, mutate, and differ from person to person and context to context.'"

THE SOUL AS AN IDEA

"'Now let us apply this distinction to our previous discussion of body and soul. To which of the two groups would body and soul belong?'

"'That is obvious, Socrates,' replied Sebastian. 'The body is visible, we perceive it through our senses, and it is changing in time. The soul, by contrast, is invisible, it never changes, and we can comprehend it only through itself, through self-consciousness.'

"'We are the result of an unhappy marriage between body and soul. Each attempts to pull the other in an opposite direction that runs contrary to its nature. When the soul attempts to understand the world, the body pushes the soul to the world of ever-changing unstable things to which it is unaccustomed. The constant bombardment of the mind by the senses confuses it. The senses make the soul nauseous, like when we are in a state of intoxication. But when the soul begins to reflect and comprehend by itself, divorced from its body, secluded from its constant nagging and pestering, then it is able to gain knowledge of its proper realm, of the pure, eternal, and unchangeable ideas. This is the realm where the soul dwells in comfort, where it belongs, with other entities that resemble it. We call this state of nirvana *wisdom*. This is where philosophers, lovers of wisdom, want to be.

"'When body and soul are united in what is often called life, the natural order of things is that the soul rules and directs the body. The soul tells the body where to go and what to do. When the body makes demands to satisfy its needs and desires, the soul decides if, when, and how to satisfy them. In a proper union of body and soul, the soul governs and the body obeys.

"'The relationship between God and man is often presented as similar to the relationship between the soul and the body. Of course, one can be the reflection of the other. We may project ourselves on the divine, or God may have created us in such a way as to parallel our relationship to it. Be that as it may, the soul is the part of us that partakes in the divine; it is immortal, rational, uniform; it cannot be destroyed, and it cannot change. The body is like mortal humans: irrational, of many changing forms, and vulnerable to destruction.'

"Sebastian nodded but added, 'You already warned Simms not to interfere with your dialogue, which is increasingly turning into a monologue. But let me just point out, as an observation rather than a criticism, that what you have been outlining formed the basis for European culture until the seventeenth century, when, during the scientific revolution, scientists ceased despising the senses and the information they offered us. This new approach to the senses led, then, to the founding of empirical science. The dualistic distinction you propose between body and soul, when fused with later Judaic monotheism (which, during the biblical period, did not include a developed concept of life after death) and with the Persian Zoroastrian belief in cool heaven and hot hell, formed the Christian synthesis that lasts until today.

"'Your concept of life after death is still very different from the religious concepts because it is abstract and impersonal. You do not propose personal survival of souls with individual identities, personal memories, and so on that can continue to exist after death, pretty much as they did before it while united with their bodies. This aspect of your philosophy is not accepted in Christianity, which has a more Persian view of life after death, where righteous people enjoy life in a beautiful garden with trees while the evil people are punished in a scorching hot place.'

"'Historical perspective is always interesting, Sebastian,' said Socrates, 'but now it is time to return to our dialogue. The body gradually dissipates and disappears after death. This is a long process, and not all parts decay equally fast. The bones decay more slowly than the flesh, for example. This is the inevitable end of all corporeal things. But the invisible soul persists unchanged and passes on to another world, which, like the soul, is invisible, indeed insensible but also pure, superior to our world, and abstract, where a good and wise God is present. God willing, that is where I will be very soon. If I am right and this world is where the soul is coming from and where it is going to return to, the soul is not destroyed together with the body; it is released from it to a better and higher mode of being. The soul's attachment to the body is like an arranged marriage, it is performed against its will. At its first opportunity to leave the body, the soul is happy to depart and come unto itself, like a spouse in an unhappy marriage who can finally return to his parental home.

"'The philosophical soul is particularly ready for death. The philosopher attempts throughout life to separate, isolate, and protect the soul from the body and its distractions. The practice of philosophy is in a sense the practice of death, the separation of the soul from the body. For this reason, philosophers are ready to pass through death calmly and without much fuss. Death, to a philosopher, is like a tournament in which an athlete participates after training for years diligently and strenuously. It is the real thing, finally, yet there is really nothing new in it. Philosophy, in this respect, can be considered to be prolonged training to die.

"'Once the soul departs to an invisible world, it dwells with other things like itself: immortal, divine, and rational. The soul is finally freed of mistakes, stupidity, and folly, as well as from emotions, like fear and desire. It is no wonder myths promise that, after death, the soul can reach a most noble type of happiness or bliss as it dwells with the gods. What do you think, friends?'

"'I think you invented a beautiful vision. This must be a philosopher's heaven, disembodied and abstract, a genuine alternative to the eternal hunting fields of Native Americans, the gardens of the Middle Eastern religions, and the wild Valhalla of the Germans. If only it were true, beyond any doubt.'

"Socrates ignored Sebastian's comment and went on. 'Not all souls are as ready to die as those of philosophers who have been training for this moment all their lives. Some souls are polluted by their bodies. They are not pure and abstract and separate from their bodies when they die. These souls serve their bodies rather than the other way round. They are enchanted by their bodies, by their desires, passions, and pleasures. I am talking about the souls of such people as bodybuilders, fashion models, pornography actors, and the fans of such individuals. These souls think through their bodies rather than their minds. This makes them think that only what can be perceived through the senses can be true. Things they cannot see, hear, touch, taste, drink, or have intercourse with do not exist for them; they cannot recognize them as true. This includes much of what philosophy is about: justice, beauty, and abstract concepts in general. Such souls are afraid, hate, and attempt to suppress what they cannot see and comprehend. These are the sort of people who hate philosophy and find it unintelligible. How do you think such souls confront death?'

"'With great difficulty, I should presume,' said Sebastian.

"'That is putting it mildly. Such souls are not ready. They are contaminated by their attachment to everything physical. They cannot let go of the flesh. They are afraid of having no body because they cannot imagine a form of existence that is not corporeal.

"'If I wanted to represent such souls artistically, I would make a statue that is heavy and crude, rooted, earthly, and visible, like a chunk of soil with roots that is too heavy to be lifted but stands there too visible to be ignored. A soul contaminated by the body cannot lift itself to reach escape velocity from the visible to the invisible world. The body keeps pulling it down back to the visible world. Such souls give rise to legends and folktales about ghosts and goblins. Ghosts are metaphorical representations of souls that are weighed down by their materiality. They are semi-visible, they wander the visible world from which they cannot escape, and they are scary because they are scared themselves to leave the physical world. Ghosts have no inner life, no reflections on their own condition, no philosophical abstract thoughts. When they are represented in literature or film as conversing with the living, the topics of conversation are always the world of the living, which the ghosts wish to affect or learn about somehow, never their own world, because they have none.'

"'I have seen some of those ghosts; frequently they are guests on the *Jerry Springer* show—you know, the trash TV program that interviews people who seem interested only in sex and food in large quantities and irrespective of quality,' interjected Sebastian.

"'Indeed, those people are good examples of ghosts and ghouls,' agreed Socrates. 'Such souls are clearly inferior; they lack any philosophical virtue, any wisdom. They wander this world like ghosts searching for something they cannot find in places like shopping malls and fast-food joints because they are too mired in the needs and passions of their bodies to be able to rise to a spiritual level where they can consider truth and beauty and justice and other ideas. Such ghosts cannot rise above their nature, pick up a book, take a class, start thinking, or develop their character. Generally, they are controlled entirely by their passions without having any control over them, may they be for sex, power, money, or food. If the Hindus are right and the souls of the dead can be reborn as other animals, they will be reborn as donkeys. No?'

"'Or more likely as pigs,' suggested Sebastian.

"'And what of violent bullies who practice injustice and behave tyrannically, whether toward members of their family, their employees, or anybody else they sense is weak and lacks protection? I mean the kind of psychopaths who join and serve totalitarian regimes like fascists and communists—how will they be reborn?'

"'They will be reborn as animals that feed on the carcasses of dead animals, like hyenas. This is their true nature and where they belong.'

"'What about happy people who are good citizens and behave virtuously because this is how they were educated and are used to behaving and not because they are good people who, through philosophical consideration, discovered what is good, just, and virtuous and chose to behave accordingly? Such people are lucky to live in a civilized society that gave them a good education and instilled in them good social norms, for in a different society they would not have known better than to follow unreflectively its norms, however atrocious. Such conformists formed the backbone of mass totalitarian political movements such as Nazism and communism; they just followed orders and behaved as everybody else did. In a sense, they were unlucky, because in our society, they would have become accountants and dentists, pillars of their churches, and members of the PTA in their suburban neighborhoods.'

"'Why do you think such spineless conformists are happy?' inquired Sebastian.

"'Because if their souls are reborn, they will be reincarnated as social and disciplined animals, like bees, termites, or ants. Totalitarian thinkers also conceived human societies as organic entities, like beehives, where the individual is insignificant and expendable because only the hive counts in the struggle for survival and domination. It is only right that such conformists, who feel comfortable in any crowd, should be reincarnated as worker bees.

"'Only philosophers, whose souls are pure and devoid of any physical contamination when they leave the body, can reach and remain in the divine invisible realm, where they can dwell in the company of ideas. This is the reason for the otherworldliness of philosophers, why they abstain from involvement in day-to-day affairs and are not interested in becoming rich or powerful, either in business or politics. Philosophers are not particularly risk-averse or afraid of poverty and the ruin of their families if they lose their investments in business, as are greedy people who lust for money and are afraid of losing it. Philosophers do not avoid politics because they are afraid of the risks of political life, of losing their good reputation and being dishonored, like people with a passion for authority and prestige. They just do not care for power and money.'

"'That is very true, Socrates. Smart people who want to become wealthy and powerful have better avenues to reach such goals than through philosophy. I advise my students to go to law school.'

"'Sound advice. If they are not good enough to become philosophers and gain wisdom, they can at least gain wealth or power and take care of their families by becoming successful lawyers,' agreed Socrates. 'Philosophers are distinctive from others for caring first and foremost for their souls and not for external, insignificant matters like wealth and power. Philosophers want to separate their souls from the demands of their bodies and dissociate themselves from people who care more for wealth and power than their souls. They follow Philosophy, a guiding goddess, on the road toward purification and care for their souls. Philosophy in that sense is a liberation movement of the soul from the body.'

"Sebastian seemed to be a little confused about Socrates's personification of philosophy as a goddess who personally leads the philosopher down a road, so Socrates elaborated. 'We live in a kind of prison that we constructed for ourselves. The body chains our souls inside this prison; it does not allow our soul to escape and see the world for what it really is. All we can do is try to glimpse at it through the bars on our prison window. Our imprisonment is painful, for we are all covered in ignorance. Our prison is made of our own desires and passions and fears. Philosophy then comes to our rescue. Philosophy helps the prisoners understand the state of their captivity. Gently, gently she gives us advice and tries to help us free ourselves from the prison we constructed. She starts with a critique of the senses, of the information our eyes and ears send us. She demonstrates how deceptive sense perceptions often are. She then convinces us slowly to use our senses only when absolutely necessary and to rely instead on reason. The more the soul is separated from the body and the senses—keeping itself to itself—the more knowledge we have of true reality. Philosophy teaches the imprisoned soul to not trust the senses—what is visible and tactile—but to trust only the invisible abstract conceptual intuitions that reason comes up with by itself, such as our study of the ideas of justice or beauty or truth. The truly philosophical soul understands that its deliverance from the confines of the prison is through abstaining as much as possible from physical pleasures, desires, pains, and fears, and bringing them under control, for they are the bars that create the prison of the soul. When people are concerned about their physical pleasures and pains and the inevitably adjacent fears of pains and loss of pleasures, they suffer a much greater harm than if their fears were realized, and they lose, for example, their good health or their property.'

"'What is this greatest harm, Socrates?' asked Sebastian.

"'Pleasure and pain confuse us about what is real. What seems to cause us the greatest pleasure or pain appears to be the most "real." For example, if a part of the body causes great pain, all our thoughts are on that part of the body because it appears to be the most real thing; we ignore other things and believe in what seems to be the source of the pain. But this belief is often false. You may have heard of the medical phenomenon of phantom limb, when people who lose a limb continue to feel its presence and sense that it is painful or itching. What appears to cause us pleasure or pain may not be real, yet pain and pleasure deceive us to believe that it is.

"'Pleasure and pain and fear, then, are the most powerful tools of bondage that can enslave the soul to the body. Each pleasure and each pain is another nail that hammers the soul down to the body and prevents it from escaping its dungeon. With each pleasure and pain, the body forces the soul to bend and accept as true whatever the body throws at it. If the soul accepts its pleasures and pains as those of the body, it begins to increasingly resemble the body and gradually becomes indistinguishable from it, fully bonded and imprisoned. It cannot rise to the invisible high realm of pure ideas. Since the realm of unchanging ideas is what is real, remaining imprisoned in the confines of the senses prevents the soul from having any idea of true reality.

"'Philosophers, the true lovers of wisdom, must always exercise self-control and courage. Otherwise, all their efforts to separate their souls from their bodies and elevate them to the level of pure ideas will be undone by the body. Philosophy can set us free from the body, release us from its prison. But pleasure and pain can quickly reverse these achievements and return the philosopher to the bondage of the body, like a slave who escapes a cruel master only to return to bondage out of his fears of freedom and longing for what is familiar. The slave would have to break free again and again, locked into endless cycles of bondage and escape, like Oprah Winfrey's continual weight-loss and weight-gain cycles. Self-control can calm desire like an antacid can settle an upset stomach. Then the soul can follow reason and remain free, dwelling in truth, ideas, and what we call the divine. This is the kind of life the philosophical soul likes to live while it is alive. Then, after death, it hopes to be fully freed of all the ills of the body, its pleasures and pains, and to finally dwell among other entirely invisible and abstract entities. The soul goes home, as it were. For this reason, dear Simms and Sebastian, a philosopher has nothing to fear from death. Death is not the end. Death is not a trip to a foreign, faraway, strange, and dark country. Death is a homecoming.'

"Socrates's evocative, rhetorically impressive, and metaphorically imaginative and rich exposition left us speechless. Everybody was quiet for a while as we mentally digested what Socrates had said, then we subjected his opinions and arguments to critical analysis. Even Socrates himself seemed to be pondering what he had just said. Sebastian and Simms were speaking to each other in low tones. Noticing them, Socrates asked them to share with us their thoughts, especially if they had found any weakness, mistake, or incompleteness in his argument. He told us he realized there must be much to question and criticize about what he had said, if anyone cared to analyze it thoroughly.

"'If you are discussing something else, excuse the interruption. But if you have doubts about my argument, please do not hesitate: share them with us; tell us exactly what is on your mind. If I can be of any use in responding to your concerns, please allow me to be of service in the few hours that are left to me.'

"'Well, to be honest,' said Simms, 'Sebastian and I have some doubts and questions. But we have been reluctant to challenge you in your current situation. Somebody who is about to die in a few hours and has developed an optimistic theory about what awaits him in an afterlife may not want to entertain doubts about it. We do not want to upset you. So we have been urging each other in whispers to raise our doubts and questions, which we have been reluctant to voice ourselves.'

"Socrates burst laughing. 'Oh, boo, death, scary, do not upset the unfortunate dying man and the mourners. Bring in the violins and the tissues. Death should be a solemn and sad occasion; very respectable, very proper, no doubts or questions or disrespect for the dead and dying, start playing the requiems now already, hey? Humbug! I have been trying to convince you for the past few hours that philosophers have nothing to fear from death. There is no reason for a philosopher to be sad about knowing he or she is about to die, quite the contrary. If I have not succeeded in convincing you, a couple of accomplished philosophers, and thereby releasing you from a childish fear of, and reluctance to discuss, death, whom can I expect to convince?!'

"Sebastian and Simms lowered their heads, ashamed of their reluctance to challenge Socrates's argument just because he was about to die.

"Socrates continued. 'This discussion is my swan song. As the legend goes, swans, just before they die, are given the gift of prophecy and know they are about to die. Facing their impending death, they sing their most beautiful songs out of happiness, knowing they are about to depart this world and go to a better one. Humans who are afraid of death project their fears onto the poor swans and slander them, claiming their beautiful last song is a mourning song for their fate. But this cannot be true. Everybody knows that birds do not sing when they are sad or in pain, not even the nightingale. I believe that the swan's song is an ode to joy, a happy anticipation of good things to come after death. The closest thing in music is Fauré's Requiem, a lullaby for death. I am not only an ugly duckling but also a swan, and, like a swan, I know what awaits me after death, and so this last discussion is my joyful swan song. So please stop worrying about upsetting me and ask all your questions, however upsetting they may seem to you, before I must rush to my happy appointment with death.'

"Simms appeared relieved and grateful. He suggested that he would present his arguments against Socrates's theory first, and then Sebastian would raise his own objections. Addressing Socrates, he said they had to acknowledge first how difficult it is to discuss and reach probable conclusions about what the invisible soul is and about death and what may or may not come after it from the perspective of people who are still embodied in corporeal bodies in this visible world.

"'Still, since these questions are very important, we must ponder them from every possible perspective and pursue them doggedly until we reach one of two conclusions: either we find out the truth for ourselves, through personal intuition and insight or through the convincing arguments of other people. If that is impossible, we must settle for an inferior type of knowledge, find the best theory available even if it is less than certain, and use it as a kind of temporary lifeboat or scaffold that respectively carries us through the sea of life or holds the structure of our lives, until we find a more solid foundation for our beliefs and can pull down the scaffolds once the edifice of our knowledge is able to stand on its own firm foundations.

"'Having said all that, and taking into consideration your earlier encouragement to use the time left to raise any doubt we may have about your theory and not to give any consideration to your current situation or even to respect you as a mentor, I will say exactly what I think. I find your explanation inadequate!'

"'You may well be right, old buddy,' Socrates encouraged, 'but please be precise and tell me exactly which points of my theory you find inadequate.'

"'You described the soul as invisible, immaterial, beautiful, and even divine. If we consider the mind or consciousness, it is always invisible but not always beautiful or divine. When the body is in some kind of imbalance, under the influence of all sorts of mind-altering substances, or when the brain is damaged in an accident, or when we are dehydrated and suffer from delusions, the mind is affected. The mind, consciousness, can then be said to supervene on the body. That is to say, any change at the level of the mind means there is also a change at the level of the body. But not every change in the body causes a change in the mind. The same experience at the level of the mind can be affected by different physical processes, just as the experience of pain alleviation can result from taking medications like aspirin or Tylenol® that work on entirely different parts of the brain. Not all physical changes in the body cause a change in our state of mind; for example, what I have for lunch does not affect my mind. But all changes in our mind require physical changes in the body; any thought or emotion has a physical manifestation.

"'Now, if our mind, our consciousness, supervenes on the brain, when the body is destroyed, the mind is destroyed as well; consciousness shuts off, as it were. You can think of the mind as the screen of a computer. We see all sorts of things on the screen that have different properties from those of the digital processes that take place behind the screen. Different types of computers, software, and digital processes may generate the same screens. But if the power supply to the computer is shut off, or if the hard disk is destroyed, the screen will go blank. Death can be just like that. When the particular constellations of the body and its brain that allow consciousness to emerge cease to hold when the body is destroyed, consciousness is turned off.'

"Socrates was clearly happy with Simms's argument, knowing it would lead to a good debate and discussion. He opened his eyes wide and looked around, as was his manner, and with a smile said, 'Simms is quite right to make this valid and complex argument. It is a genuine alternative to what I had proposed. This is so good, I may need some help. Can one of you who is smarter than me attempt to answer Simms's arguments on my behalf? Maybe in the meantime, while we gather our thoughts, we can hear Sebastian's critical comments. We can then compare Simms's arguments with Sebastian's and reflect on them both. If both are right, we will have to accept their conclusions. If not, we can argue with them and have a good time debating further.' Turning to Sebastian, Socrates invited him to present his doubts.

"Sebastian said, 'To be honest, it appears to me as if your argument has not progressed much since my last criticism. I asked you to prove not just that the soul precedes birth but that it also outlasts the body. If I accept what you said about the preexistence of the soul, before life, I still do not have to accept that the soul also exists after death. Allow me to distinguish my argument from that of Simms here: unlike Simms, I am ready to admit that the soul is stronger and can endure longer than the body. Your argument seems to be that, since the soul has a more lasting nature than the body, it must outlast its weaker companion. But the stronger does not always survive the weaker in every instance. For example, compare a baker to a loaf of bread that she bakes. Obviously, the baker is stronger and more durable than the bread. Bread can only last for a few days before it spoils. During a lifetime, the baker must bake thousands of loaves of bread. But suppose that one day, after the baker finished baking the bread, she dies. There in front of us is the fresh bread and the dead baker. But then somebody, let's call him Socrates, comes along and says that the baker cannot be dead, because there in front of her is a fresh loaf of bread, and the baker must be stronger and longer-lasting than any loaf of bread. If anybody argues with him, this Socrates would ask which is longer-lasting, bakers or loaves of bread. This Socrates will then guide his interlocutor to reach the inevitable conclusion that the dead baker must still be alive.

"'The relationship between soul and body may resemble that of the baker to the loaf of bread she baked. The soul is stronger and longer-lasting than the body. Every soul may consume many bodies, as the baker may consume countless loaves of bread in a long life. Each of these loaves will last only a few days before the baker bakes and eats another loaf. But one day, there will be a loaf that the baker will not consume because she will die first. Likewise, the soul may die at a certain point, and the body would then die immediately after it. Even if we grant you the reincarnation theory of souls—that souls may outlive the body and be reincarnated in another body and then outlive that body only to be reincarnated again and again—this does not prove that, at the end of one of the reincarnations, the soul might not wear itself out and die in the sense of ceasing to exist and not in the sense of being released from the body.

"'If some souls survive the death of the body, they may be able to tell us about it, carry information about the experience and what follows it. But souls that entirely cease to exist cannot tell. Therefore, I think there is no basis for your confidence that any particular death of the body will not be accompanied by the death of the soul. You offered no reason to believe that the soul is immortal and cannot perish. Therefore, a person who is about to die may have reason to fear that perhaps this time the soul will perish along with the body and will not be released for continued existence on a higher and better level, as you seem to be confident will happen.'"

BACK IN BINGHAMTON:
THE DARK SIDE OF ARGUING

After Fred and Cheryl had finished their meal, Fred ordered coffee and told Cheryl, "Simms and Sebastian were very convincing. It was embarrassing because I wanted Socrates and his argument to win. He was going to die soon, and he had this nice theory that promised him a philosophical existence beyond the grave, the kind that might not seem very interesting to people who put their physical pleasures first, but for a philosopher, Socrates's theory promised him an interesting future. Simms and Sebastian had made us feel uncertain and insecure. Later, after Socrates's death, I discussed this with the others who had been present, and they all told me that they had had the same feelings of unease about the theory and compassion toward Socrates. We also felt insecure about our own conclusions, because we were all fans of Socrates and usually agreed with him."

"I am right there with you," said Cheryl, who had followed Fred's narration of Socrates's final discussion very intently. "As you were describing Simms and Sebastian's counterarguments, I was wondering how Socrates could possibly answer them. Socrates's argument was very convincing at the beginning, but then it seems to have been crushed. I have to admit that Simms's theory about the supervenience of the mental on the physical has always had a great attraction for me. I am not a philosopher of mind, but as you described Simms's position, that theory came back to me, and now I have to consider it as my own position. I would have to agree with Simms that the soul dies, consciousness ends, and the mind ceases to exist with the body. But tell me, please, how did Socrates continue the discussion? Did he also feel insecure and doubtful, and was he consequently sad, as he was about to die very soon? Or did he take the criticism in stride and calmly gave a satisfying answer? Go on, tell me what happened next."

Fred smiled, remembering Socrates's response. "Like you, dear Cheryl, I also admired Socrates as a person and even more so as a debater and a philosopher. But I have never admired him more than at that moment. Of course he was able to give an answer. There was nothing extraordinary about that. But you should have observed his calmness, how gentle and pleasant and encouraging he was. He treated the criticisms of the two younger philosophers with respect and support. He considered their ability to criticize his position and argument so well under those circumstances as a great achievement, proof of the success of the kind of education he had imparted to them. He treated them as his philosophical equals and considered their arguments carefully, then replied to them dispassionately. He was like a leader rallying his troops after their line had been broken by the enemy and they retreated. Once more into the breach, he would call, rallying them to his flag to attack and turn the tide of battle."

Cheryl urged Fred on. Thrilled by the suspense, she wanted to know immediately how the debate continued to unfold.

"I was sitting next to Socrates as he whispered to me, 'Don't give up Sergeant Fred. We will regroup and you will lead the charge.' I told him he was my officer and that I would follow him into battle. But he explained to me that in this battle, rank would matter little. 'We are all foot soldiers,' he said, 'and it does not matter who runs first and who follows.' Socrates then warned me against the first danger we were likely to encounter, a kind of minefield before the actual battle.

"'Which danger?' I asked.

"'The danger of coming to hate and mistrust rationality and

the power of argument,' he answered. 'To use fashionable ter-minology, I see danger in the desire to deconstruct and dismiss any argument or rational deduction and inference as "logo-centric." This fear and hatred of rationality and argumentation is akin to misanthropy, the fear and hatred of other people. If you put them both together, you get the fear and hatred of "anthropomorphism," another frightening word that means putting people at the center of philosophical inquiry and understanding everything in such subjective human terms, as I do. The reason for all these fears and hatreds is the same: igno-rance of the complexity of the world we live in.

"'Misanthropy, the hatred of people, results from overcon-fidence in people. An inexperienced person trusts another without sufficient reason as being good, honest, and faithful. Then there is disappointment. The trusted person is discovered to be unreliable, a liar, perhaps a crook, even a psychopath. Then the same unfortunate experience repeats itself. When this happens within one's inner circle of family, close friends, and confidants, it is easy for that person to conclude that all people are untrustworthy and wicked and that nobody is any good; thus the person begins to hate the whole of humanity. The reason for this is that when we have to deal with other people, we often do not know and cannot know what kind of people they are. Had we known, we would have been able to know whom to trust and whom to distrust. We would probably figure out that few people deserve trust without reservation and few are wicked and are entirely untrustworthy. Most people are somewhere in between.'

"I agreed, as statistics, especially of human populations, uses many distribution models that are bell-shaped.

"'Let's put it another way,' suggested Socrates. 'If there had been a world championship in wickedness, and somebody like

Hitler had won the gold medal, how tough would it have been to compete with him? How many people would have been close to his level of wickedness?'

"'Only very few,' I replied.

"'Arguments are not exactly like people,' conceded Socrates. 'I got carried away by an interesting observation about misanthropy. But the original analogy I drew between people who distrust rationality and people who distrust other people is still enlightening. When a philosophical novice with little or no experience in making inferences and connecting evidence with arguments is convinced of the validity of some argument and then loses faith in the argument for good or bad reasons—whether the argument is valid or false—and then the same thing happens to that person again and again with other arguments, such a person loses any faith in any argument, in the very ability of human reason to rationally understand and interpret the world. Every once in a while you meet such people. It usually starts when they read the work of a particular philosopher, like Marx or Rawls or Strauss or Rand (the politics does not matter here, only the charisma) and are naively enthusiastic, believing that this one philosopher has solved all the problems of both philosophy and life. They become faithful disciples and evangelists rather than critical philosophers. Then, when they learn more about philosophy and life, they see how weak some of the arguments and conclusions really are. They also learn just how many other alternative arguments exist. They may go through a personal crisis and as a result lose their faith in philosophy altogether. Many of the postmodernist classics were written by people who believed in Marxism. Then, when they discovered again and again the weakness of the Marxist arguments, they became disillusioned with philosophy in general and with the ability of reason and rational arguments to resolve any issue.

Such people develop ironic detachment from any argument and any claim for truth. Then they delude themselves that they are the smartest members of the philosophical tribe because they, and they alone, can see how futile the whole attempt to reason is. They come to believe that arguments are nothing but ideological subterfuges by powerful interests to manipulate unsuspecting audiences. Like politicians, public relations specialists, and lawyers, they come to believe that equally good arguments can be brought or invented on both sides of any issue.

"'But there are good arguments out there that can lead us to the truth. Human reason is able to sift through evidence and distinguish valid from invalid arguments and then reach the truth. It is a pity that, when people are exposed to a bad argument they believe to be true and then discover it to be false, instead of blaming themselves and their insufficient experience and education in valid argumentation and solid inference, they transfer the blame from themselves to human reason and argumentation in general. Then they come to hate and deride philosophy and logical argument for the rest of their lives.'

"As I was one of the least experienced philosophers there who also spoke French, I was most in danger of succumbing to the temptation to ditch philosophy and logical argument as 'modern logocentric meta-narratives.'

"'We must be careful, first and foremost,' he told me, 'not to internalize that there is no truth and no good argument that can deduce or infer it. If an argument we accept as sound is proven wrong, let us conclude that the fault was with us, that we made some mistake that we can and should correct. Next time we will make a better argument; if we are wrong again, we will be wrong in a better way, more intelligently, then we will try again, until we get as close to the truth as we possibly can. The fault is not in philosophical argument as such. You will see, dear Fred, that as you learn from your mistakes and from the objections others make to your arguments, your arguments will become better and better, sounder, more sophisticated, and better able to anticipate possible objections.

"'A philosopher experienced in arguing, as I am, may fall prey to a different kind of mistake: to treat debates like a competitive sport rather than an open-ended search for truth. A philosopher, unlike an athlete, should not care about winning contests. In philosophy, winning is the discovery of the truth, which can be shared by all. But if accomplished debaters forget that they are philosophers, they may want to win the argument on their technical skills alone, even though the result is not the discovery of the truth but the vacuous demonstration of technical superiority of one trained philosopher over another. Philosophy is not a competitive spectator sport in which each competitor attempts to impress an audience with superior performance and win applause. I have to be careful because at this moment, facing death, I have to admit that the only difference between me and the technical debater who seeks to convince an audience rather than find the truth may be that I wish to convince only myself of the truth of my argument; convincing the audience here is of secondary significance for me. If my argument about the soul and life after death is true, then it is good for me to believe in the truth. If it is not true and death is the end, it will still do me good to believe in the immortality of the soul in the little time that is left for me to live because it will comfort my friends to believe that I am not coming to an end, and that my own ignorance of the truth will last only briefly, before it ends along with everything else about me.'"

CRITICAL DISCUSSION

"Socrates then turned to Simms and Sebastian and addressed them directly: 'I gave you a fair warning about my biases regarding the topics we are arguing about. But I order and beseech you to think of the truth first and foremost, and not about Socrates. You should express agreement with me only if you think I make a valid argument for the truth. If not, you must argue against me with all guns blazing, so that I may not deceive you as well as myself due to my strong personal interest in proving the immortality of the soul. Do not let me poison you with self-deception before I die, like a bee that leaves its stinger in its victim before it dies.

"'So let's get on with it. First, let me summarize your main arguments to be sure I have understood you. Please correct me if I misrepresent you. Simms considers the soul to be added onto the body. He thinks that, although it may have higher emergent properties like consciousness, it may still die with the body. Sebastian, unlike Simms, accepts that the soul may outlive the body. But he claims that even if the soul goes through several cycles of physical birth, life, death, rebirth, and so on, it may still come to an end as one of those cycles comes to a close and die together with the body. Are these your main arguments?'

"Simms and Sebastian accepted Socrates's summing up of their counterarguments.

"'These arguments are inconsistent with some of what I have argued earlier, most notably, with the theory of knowledge as recollection: that the soul learned things before it was born into a body, and that when we come to know things, the soul actually remembers the ideas or concepts it acquainted itself with prior to joining a body in this life. If this theory is correct, the soul must have existed in some other realm before it joined a body. Both Sebastian and Simms seem to have accepted this theory of knowledge.

"'But this theory of knowledge is inconsistent with Simms's claim that the soul is added onto the body. Knowledge must reside in the mind, and so it cannot precede what the mind is added to; in this case, the body. A mind that is added to the body comes into being and disappears with that body; it cannot precede it. So when and where does the added mind acquire the memories that can later generate knowledge?'

"'You are right, Socrates,' conceded Simms. 'I am either committed to rejecting your recollection theory of knowledge, or I have to come up with a way for the body to exist before the human organism is formed, for example, in the genetic material that makes a person but predates that person, being the result of a very long evolutionary process.'

"'Let us discuss, then, your suggested relationship between this adding and the mind or soul and the body. There can be no change at the "upper" added level—the mind, in this case—without a change at the "lower" added-upon level—the body.'

"'That is right,' said Simms. 'This is the definition of supervenience or adding.'

"'The mind cannot act then, cannot cause anything or be affected by anything independently of the body; there has to a physical change at the level of the body, like in the brain.'

"Simms agreed again. 'This is also derived from the definition of supervenience.'

"'If so, the mind cannot control the body, because changes in the mind cannot happen without physical changes, but changes in the body can cause changes in the mind?'

"'That is correct.'

"'So it must also be impossible for mind and body to clash because every change in the mind must imply a change in the body?'

"'No clashes, no conflicts; they are the same thing,' affirmed Simms.

"'OK, now, presumably, if the doctrine of supervenience is correct, a certain constellation or constellations of physical states correspond with consciousness, the mind, what we can also call the soul?'

"'Yes,' agreed Simms. 'Note that the physical constellations from which conscious minds emerge can be very different from each other; they do not even need to be organic. Consciousness could also emerge from inorganic matter, as could be the case with a very sophisticated computer in the future.'

"'We can agree that consciousness is the hallmark of the mind or the soul. The world can be divided into two types of things, conscious and unconscious, with nothing in between, like half a mind or a third of a consciousness.'

"Simms agreed again.

"'Now tell me, Simms, don't we say about some souls that they possess goodness and intelligence and are therefore good, and about others that they are stupid and wicked and are therefore bad?'

"'Obviously.'

"'Explain to me, then, how do supporters of the supervenience theory of mind explain moral or value-laden properties of the soul like goodness and badness? Would they have to say that goodness or badness supervene on some physical properties that give rise to such moral qualities?'

"'Yes,' said Simms. 'I do not know exactly how, but I suppose that any defender of the supervenience thesis would have to say something of this sort.'

"'But this seems inconsistent with what we have just agreed on, that there is no gradation in consciousness or mind. Either you have it or you do not. By contrast, goodness and wickedness come in degrees. Goodness and wickedness are also moral categories. At least some philosophers argue that they assume some degree of free will. Now how do such moral qualities of the soul supervene on physical properties?'

"'Well, Socrates,' conceded Simms, 'nobody knows exactly how the mind may supervene on the body and how consciousness emerges. The answers, if there are any, to your questions will have to come from neuroscience or some other science of the mind, not from philosophy. So I cannot answer these questions now.'

"'Fine, we will have to leave these doubts aside for now. But tell me: what governs our behavior, especially when we are philosophers, the soul or the body? For example, the body may tell us that it is very thirsty and lead us to water, yet the soul may stop it, and the same with hunger and myriad other physical impulses that we have but are stopped by the wise soul that governs the body. Generally, we have all experienced numerous times our soul or mind ordering our body to do this or that against its will and, more so, against its passions and desires. Now, if the mind supervenes on the body, it cannot cause it to do anything, because any change in the higher level of the mind also requires a change in the lower level of the body, but not vice versa. Unless and until you offer a convincing account of mental causation, your supervenience theory runs counter to our everyday experience of our mental life. You end up with an inconsistent view of our mental life.

"'So much for supervenience,' concluded Socrates. 'Now, what kind of argument can I bring against Sebastian's counterargument?'

"'Oh, I trust you to find a way to pull the rug out from under my argument,' Sebastian chuckled. 'I was surprised that you had such interesting criticisms of Simms's argument for supervenience. I did not expect them. Before I listened to you, his argument sounded so convincing. I expect my argument to suffer the same fate. But please make it short and painless.'

"'Oh, no, dear friend,' replied Socrates. 'Overconfidence can be just as fatal for an argument as ignorance.

"'Permit me to summarize once more your argument, so we are all reminded of it and you can guarantee that I do not misrepresent you. You want me to prove that the soul is immortal and cannot perish. You think it is foolish of an old philosopher who is about to die to confidently believe that his soul will survive death and will even prosper more than the souls of people who have not devoted their lives to philosophy. You say that demonstrating that the soul existed before the body and is of a nobler nature than the body does not guarantee its immortality. The soul may live longer than any body, and we may remember its previous existence when we come to know ideas that do not exist in this visible world but in an invisible world where the soul may have existed previously and come into contact with ideas, but it still does not mean that it will continue to exist after this body perishes. The soul may, in a sense, be infected by the body, just like when a parasite settles in an organism: it tires out the organism and draws its energy until it dies. Similarly, the body may be a kind of disease that infects the soul with material existence and eventually kills it. It does not matter if there is reincarnation of souls or not, because even if there is, this current incarnation may be the last one. We simply cannot know. Do you have anything to add to this summary of your opinion, or do you wish to subtract anything?'

"'No, that is a fair representation of my position.'

"Socrates seemed to be lost in reflection. He addressed Sebastian again: 'Replying to your argument requires an extensive and thorough discussion that goes beyond the limited scope of the issue of the immortality of the soul. I would need to get into a discussion of the general reasons for the generation and death of anything. This is a serious and difficult topic, but I believe that after I develop the general theory, we will be able to apply it to the particular problem of human life, and perhaps then reply to your objection.'"

HOW DID SOCRATES BECOME A PHILOSOPHER?

"Socrates appeared for the first time to be as old as he actually was. He started reminiscing about his intellectual life and formation. 'When I was a young man,' he began, 'my first love was not philosophy but natural science. My first major in college was science. It seemed to me at the time that natural science might have the deepest and surest knowledge, so if I really wanted to understand the world, I should become a natural scientist, perhaps a physicist. My fascination with physics followed the sense I had that it could explain the causes and reasons of everything: why things are created, why they persist as they are for a while, and why they are destroyed and perish. I was interested in questions such as why do fish stink when they rot? Where do flies come from on rotten meat? Why does milk become sour? Why do all mammals have five digits and all lizards have only three? Why do zebras have stripes? Why did the dinosaurs perish? I was also interested in the grand questions of cosmology: what are the origins and destiny of the universe? Why did the big bang in which the universe is supposed to have begun happen, and will there be "big crunch" at the end?

"'Then I became convinced that I am no good for such scientific inquiries. Let me explain why. I became so fascinated with these scientific questions that I ceased to understand things that had been obvious to me earlier. I was puzzled by the simplest facts of growth and addition. I used to think like everybody else that people get fat by eating more and more, and by turning the food into fat and flesh.'

"'That is reasonable enough,' interjected Sebastian.

"'Not anymore. When I looked at two things—say, two bananas—and added them together, it was a case of $1 + 1 = 2$. Or vice versa: if one of the bananas was taken away, it was a case of $2 - 1 = 1$. But now I cannot understand how a whole of two is generated from two separate individuals. Nor can I understand how a whole of two could suddenly generate two units of one. These basic questions of what I would come to know as the philosophy of mathematics prevented me from continuing my studies of natural science.

"'Then I heard about philosophy. I learned that philosophy asks not just about the causes of things but also about their meanings. Philosophy asks not only what the cause of the universe is but also what its meaning is. This made me very excited because I thought philosophy would be able to explain why things are the way they are, why they change, and what is the purpose of it all.

"'So I changed my major to philosophy and started studying it assiduously, only to be disappointed yet again. Some philosophers had no different worldview than the scientists. They considered the world to be just a large mechanism with causes connecting one event to the next. Other philosophers accepted that we perceive the world as imbued with meaning and that this reflects our intentionality. That is to say, the closer things in the world are to what I intend them to be, the more meaningful they appear to me, and vice versa: the more irrelevant or unresponsive to my intentions things are, the more meaningless they appear to be. Some philosophers argued that we live in a world that is entirely indifferent to human intentions and appears therefore absurd. I was dissatisfied with all these philosophies because I felt that, except for the addition of human intentionality, they did not change or add much to the causal mechanistic explanation of reality.

"'Next I decided that my problem might be excessive use of my senses, which then made them unreliable. I imagined that, just like people who study the sun by looking at it directly might harm their sense of sight, I might be "burning" my senses by exposing them to objects in the world. The solution for a person who wants to study the sun during an eclipse might be to observe it indirectly, through its reflections on water or some other such reflecting materials. So instead of studying the world empirically, through the senses, I decided to seek the truth through studying ideas theoretically from my armchair. Instead of trying to study the sun through the senses, I attempted to study the idea of the sun as embedded in a theory. The analogy here is imperfect because I came to realize that the ideas are in fact much clearer and closer to the truth than the objects of our sense perceptions. The idea of the sun that can be studied theoretically is in fact clearer and truer than the sun we see through our eyes. Be that as it may, my philosophical methodology became to hypothesize first a theoretical principle or idea, which I intuited was the strongest, and then use it as a basis to find out what else must be true if this first principle were true. I rejected as untrue anything that was inconsistent with the chosen principle. But I see from your expressions that I have been running ahead of myself, and you do not quite understand what I am talking about.'

"We all nodded. We knew how difficult it must have been for Socrates to try to explain the internal turmoil that led him to evolve his philosophy.

"'What I came up with in the end is exactly what you have been hearing about this whole day today: my theory of ideas. I start with assuming a perfect absolute idea, like beauty or goodness or greatness. I assume the independent existence of these perfect ideas and then demonstrate the incredible scope of different things that they are able to explain better than any other philosophical theory I know of. They then become indispensable. I want to show that this hypothetical method—assuming a useful first principle, an idea—and following how it can solve a broad scope of problems can prove the immortality of the soul.'

"Sebastian interjected, 'Please show me, if you can, how to derive the immortality of the soul from the theory of ideas. Alas, we have so little time left to be in your company.'

"Socrates did not waste time. 'Let us consider the various beautiful things in the world, like thoroughbred horses and dogs; Angelina and Brad; structures, like the Guggenheim Museum in Bilbao, the Parthenon in Athens, and the Chrysler Building in New York City; music, like Bach's cantatas, Mozart's Requiem, Mahler's symphonies, and Pink Floyd's *Atom Heart Mother*; landscapes like the Arizona desert, the California redwood forest, the New England shore and beach in Cape Cod. What can possibly be common to all these things? What makes them beautiful? What is the reason for their beauty? In my opinion, it is their relationship to an absolute idea of beauty. Do I make myself clear?'

"'As clear as the idea of clarity itself. Please go on.'

"'I do not think there is any better alternative that explains even remotely as well the reason for why we consider such entirely different things beautiful. Any attribute you may consider, like shape or color, is not shared by all the things we consider beautiful. What else can the Chrysler Building, Angelina, and a Bach cantata have in common? The only explanation that also has the virtue of simplicity is that they all share a relationship to the absolute idea of perfect beauty. I am open to various possible formulations of this relationship: it might partake in the idea of beauty; it might imitate or reflect beauty; it might be designed by somebody like an architect who can see in his mind's eye the idea of beauty. The exact relationship between the perfect and absolute ideas and objects in this world is not important to the point I am about to make. Some other philosopher can work out those exact details after my death. I only insist that the reason for the perception of beauty we have is the idea of beauty. We somehow compare the imperfectly beautiful things we see with our eyes or hear with our ears with the one idea of beauty we see with our mind's eye, and then we conclude whether or not things are beautiful and to what degree.

"'A similar account applies to all the other ideas, like greatness. Great things are great by virtue of their relationship to the idea of greatness. Small things are small because of their relationship to the idea of smallness.

"'My theory of ideas solves problems that result from describing relationships between opposites. Think, for example, about the relationship between two people, one of whom is taller than the other, whereas the other is shorter than the first.'

"'Like Paul Simon and Art Garfunkel or Arnold Schwarzenegger and Denny DeVito?'

"'Yes, exactly. If we say that Garfunkel is taller than Simon by a foot, we also say that Simon is shorter than Garfunkel by a foot. A foot is pretty short. So if we add a short thing, a foot, to a short person, Simon, we get a tall man, Garfunkel. How can that be? How can two things that share the property of shortness, Simon and a foot, generate their opposite, the tall Garfunkel? An elegant solution that avoids this apparent absurdity is that Garfunkel and Schwarzenegger partake of the idea of tallness, whereas Simon and DeVito partake of the idea of shortness.'

"Sebastian laughed and assured Socrates that he understood the example.

"'Now let us look at numbers and the philosophy of mathematics. $1 + 1 = 2$. $6 \div 3 = 2$. What is the meaning of this number, 2, that resulted twice from our computations: once by addition and once by division? In the first equation, the reason for 2 that gives it its meaning is the addition of 1 and 1. In the second case, the reason for 2 is the division of 6 by 3. But these two meanings and reasons for 2 are different, maybe even inconsistent. How can the first 2 have the same meaning as the second one? The only explanation I can think of is the idea of 2, a perfect absolute 2 that the results of the addition and division share. This sharing in the idea of 2 makes the results of both computations "2s," just like sharing in the idea of beauty makes Brad and Angelina both pretty.

"'Ideas may also be connected to one another in a hierarchical structure. For example, being honest is good, and we know people who are honest. Being charitable is good as well, and we know people who are charitable. Each person who is charitable partakes in the idea of charity. Likewise, each person who is honest partakes in the idea of honesty. But the ideas of honesty and charity themselves partake in the higher idea of the good. Philosophers are interested in understanding the highest ideas because other ideas, lower on the hierarchy, partake in them. So, if we understand goodness, we already understand charity and honesty. Therefore, philosophers are interested in the highest ideas, like those of goodness, more than in the less abstract ones, like charity or honesty. Philosophers are more interested in the idea of the number than in the idea of individual numbers like 2 or 3. But you are philosophers, so you know what I am talking about; I do not need to convince you of what you already know.'

"Simms and Sebastian said at once that, indeed, they knew exactly what he was saying and that they were practicing the investigation of the higher ideas."

PHILOSOPHY AS THE STUDY OF THE HIGHER IDEAS

Back in Binghamton, Cheryl and Fred paid the bill. Cheryl said she was not surprised that Simms and Sebastian agreed with Socrates's characterization of the task of philosophy as understanding the higher ideas. Cheryl praised Socrates for how clearly he put forward his position. Fred agreed and added that this was also the impression of everybody who was standing at Socrates's deathbed. Despite the late hour and the circumstances, Socrates put forth his case clearly, articulately, and convincingly. Cheryl praised Fred for his rendition of the story of Socrates's last hours, saying that "the argument lost none of its articulate persuasiveness." She urged Fred to finish the story of Socrates's attempt to prove the immortality of his soul.

Fred continued. "So, there was a general agreement that the ideas exist, and that everything else receives its reason, meaning, and essence from partaking or reflecting these ideas. Socrates then raised a new issue: the relationships between ideas that are opposite of each other. We can arrange at least some ideas in pairs of opposites such as good versus evil; beautiful versus ugly; tall versus short; odd versus even; and so on. Socrates attempted to show that opposite ideas are mutually exclusive. For example, the idea of the beautiful excludes ugliness, the idea of the good excludes evil, the idea of the tall excludes the short, and so on.

By contrast, the visible objects that partake or reflect the ideas can tolerate reflecting opposite ideas.

"As you remember, Socrates was short and chubby. I am, obviously, tall and thin, while Professor Simms is of medium height. Socrates summed up our relationships: 'Simms is shorter than Fred but taller than me. There could be an apparent contradiction here because Simms is at once short, in relation to Fred, and tall, in comparison with me. While Simms can be both tall and short, the ideas of the tall and the short exclude each other. The invisible world of ideas where opposites exclude each other is the mirror image of the visible world where they can coexist as inessential properties. The tallness and the shortness of Simms are not intrinsic and essential for his essence, like, say, his philosophy. Simms is a philosopher intrinsically. His vocation does not depend on the properties of anybody else, whether there are no other philosophers in the world or whether all the people have become philosophers. It is also essential because if somebody is not a philosopher, that person cannot be Simms. By contrast, his tallness is extrinsic; if there is no Socrates, Simms is not tall. His tallness is also inessential; somebody can be Simms whether or not they are tall. If Simms suddenly started growing again in middle age and became taller than Fred, he would still be Simms.

"'Here we find another difference between the properties of ideas and the properties of objects in the world that may partake in them. All the properties of ideas are essential. Some of the properties of objects in the world may be inessential or contingent. My height and weight, color of eyes and hair, and shoe size are inessential, contingent properties. They could be otherwise, but I will still be myself. As Gulliver found out in his travels, being big or small is entirely dependent on context. By contrast, the idea of the number 4 is essentially even; if the number were odd, it would not have been 4.'

"Socrates concluded his exposition of the differences between ideas and their reflections in this world, emphasizing the absoluteness and essential nature of the properties of the ideas. Then some youthful voice from the back of the room, probably a graduate student, raised an objection. He suggested that Socrates might have been guilty of contradicting himself. At the beginning of the conversation, Socrates claimed that opposites generate each other. His example, as you may remember, was that life generates death but that death also generates life. If we assume that tall is the opposite of short, then one should generate the other. But now Socrates argued that the ideas of the tall and the short are entirely distinct and mutually exclusive.

"Socrates listened patiently until the young student finished his question. He praised the student's courage in facing a senior audience and his good recall of the details of the earlier discussion.

"'Yet,' he explained, 'there is a difference between what we discuss now and what I talked about earlier. At the beginning of the discussion, I was talking about concrete objects in the visible world. Such objects generate opposite properties from each other. Now, I have been discussing the ideas themselves that exist in an invisible realm of their own. All their properties are essential and as such exclude coexisting with their opposites or generating each other. These properties are never generated, nor do they cease to exist, and they exclude their opposites.'

"Socrates turned then to Sebastian to inquire if he was satisfied with the answer. Sebastian assured him that he was, but Socrates, probably fearing that he may have been misunderstood, proceeded to illustrate his general philosophical principles with examples. Socrates knew that the best way to be sure that people understand you when you talk in philosophical abstractions is to provide concrete examples.

"'Think of the ideas of the cold and the hot. Then think of snow and fire. Are these the same things?'

"'Of course not,' replied Sebastian. 'Fire is hot, and snow is cold; but fire is not *the* hot, and snow is not *the* cold.'

"'When snow comes into contact with heat, the two cannot coexist. When heat affects snow, it disappears, melts into water, or even evaporates as vapor. Vice versa, when cold affects fire, the latter also retreats and eventually ceases to burn. But the hot and the cold cannot coexist or generate each other.

"'I think the source of the confusion here is a linguistic ambiguity; the same word is used to mean two entirely different things. The same word is used as a noun to name the idea itself, like heat, cold, or beauty, and as an adjective to name something else that is not the idea itself but that has some of its distinguishing characteristics, like hot fire, cold ice cream, and beautiful Angelina—although these objects, fire, ice cream, and Angelina, are not identical with the ideas of heat, cold, and beauty. Accordingly, these attributes can change; fire can grow cold and die, ice cream can grow warm and melt, and Angelina can become ugly. Fire is not the opposite of cold; ice cream is not the opposite of hot, Angelina is not the opposite of ugly. Therefore, they can all generate the opposite property: all fires eventually exhaust their fuel and turn cold, all ice cream eventually melts in the mouth, and all beautiful things eventually decay and disappear. But the ideas themselves—heat, cold, and beauty—can never turn into or generate their opposites; nor can they decay and disappear. This is part of their perfection and absoluteness.'

"After Socrates clarified the distinction between ideas in general and objects that have properties that partake in these ideas, he proceeded to apply the distinction to the difference between soul and body. He attempted to prove that the soul is an idea like beauty or heat, while the body is an object that can have this property—like ice cream can be cold. If the soul is an idea, it has the characteristics of an idea. It must be absolute and eternal.

"Socrates's discussion with Sebastian took the usual form of a dialogue. He began by asking, 'What must be present in a body to make it alive?'

"Sebastian gave the traditional answer, the soul.

"'Always?'

"'Always,' affirmed Sebastian.

"Socrates had Sebastian agree that whenever the soul possesses some body, that body becomes alive, as in the traditional meaning of 'life.'

"'And what is the opposite of living, if there is one?'

"'Dying, of course.'

"'Now this is the most crucial move,' cautioned Socrates. 'If the soul is an idea, it excludes its opposite; it is perfect and absolute and eternal. This is just like beauty, as an idea, excludes ugliness, and the idea of tall excludes the idea of short. Beautiful Angelina can become ugly, although beauty cannot become ugliness. A tall man can become short, but the idea of tallness can never turn into its opposite, shortness. The live Socrates can, and indeed soon will, become dead Socrates. But the soul, as an idea, is always alive and can never turn into its opposite, death. As much as the idea of heat cannot admit cold, as much as an odd number can never be even, the soul cannot perish. The soul is imperishable; it cannot admit any perishing, and so it is immortal and eternal. And here I rest my case!'

"Sebastian paraphrased Socrates: 'If the immortal ideal, the eternal ideal, is perishable, then nothing is imperishable.'

"'Indeed,' said Socrates. 'Even the most unphilosophical and uneducated person agrees that God and the essence of life—the soul and what is immortal in general—will never perish.'

"'Sure, Socrates,' said Sebastian. 'Even the gods themselves would agree with that.'

"'Death can kill the body, but it cannot affect its opposite, the immortal soul. We can conclude then that the mortal part of man dies, whereas the immortal part does not and cannot possibly die.'

"'That the mortal dies and the immortal lives forever is immune to any doubt,' reiterated Sebastian.

"'Then we agree that the soul is immortal and imperishable, and that after death it continues to exist in another world, different in nature from this world, an invisible world of ideas and essences that can be perceived through reason alone, through our philosophically trained "mind's eye."' Socrates looked at Sebastian and Simms for signs of further doubt.

"'I have no more objections,' exclaimed Sebastian. 'But if my friend Simms or anybody else here has further counter-arguments and criticisms, I think they'd better speak out now, since the time left for any further discussion is obviously very short, and there will never be another better, more fitting time to discuss death than now, just as our friend and mentor here, Socrates, is about to die and is anxious to exhaust the topic of death and immortality.'

"'I have nothing more to say in this dialogue,' said Simms. 'I can only add that any certainty about such difficult, great, and bewildering topics as the ones we have been discussing today runs against the general weakness and limits of finite human reason as it faces the infinitude of the universe. I must admit that I cannot help feeling my own feebleness and finitude.'

"Socrates agreed. 'You are quite right, Simms. As idealist philosophers who attempt to study the eternal ideas, we must be very careful and aware of our limitations. We must use our limited reason, our mind's eye to study the ideas, the first principles we assume to explain everything else. Even when they appear to us as clear and certain, we should treat our intuitions, what our mind's eye presents us with, cautiously. We must have cautious confidence in human reason, even when it seems to offer sure and certain insight. Be that as it may, reason is all we have. So, if you do not wish to question any of the stages of the argument and discussion that brought us here, I would like to tell you of some of my speculations about the soul and the afterlife, as it draws closer and closer from hours to minutes away.'"

SOCRATES'S VISION OF THE AFTERLIFE

"'I can offer you nothing better than speculation here, and perhaps even less than that. When ordinary descriptive language fails me and I cannot find the words to describe what my mind's eye sees, I resort to metaphoric language and tell a mythical story that can only allude indirectly, metaphorically, to what I want to say but that I cannot describe in any other way.

"'Oh, friends, what if the soul is immortal? We must take good care of it! Not just for the brief time it is united with our bodies but for eternity, for the infinite time it exists. Neglecting caring for the soul has the most terrible results. If death were the end of everything, bad people would be lucky, for they would be getting rid not just of their bodies but also of their wicked souls. Since the soul is immortal, evil people are not released from their wickedness by dying. Release from evil requires becoming just and wise. As you remember, I have always held that justice is a form of knowledge because people harm their souls when they harm others unjustly, and so they would be less than just only out of ignorance. When the soul departs the body and begins its journey to the other world, the only thing it can take with it is the care it has received during life.

"'In my mythical imagination, when a person dies, an entity like their "guardian angel" directs the migration of their soul to a "place" where all the souls gather. I say a "place," but it is a metaphor; the world where souls live without bodies is not physical and so it cannot have spatial coordinates. At this place, the guide directs and escorts the souls to the next world, where they will be judged. Then the souls spend a long time in that world. How long depends on how many experiences they need to acquire in that world. When these experiences are acquired over a long time, another guide escorts the souls back to the world of the living for reincarnation.

"'But there is no interstate highway between the state of the living and the state of the souls and ideas. Between the worlds of the living and the dead, there is something like a thick forest with many roads winding through it, with many forks and inter- sections, cul-de-sacs that lead nowhere, clearings in the forests, and swamps. If a soul does not pay careful attention to its non- physical surroundings, it is easy to get lost in such a forest without a guide. A well-disciplined soul will follow its guide. A philosophical soul will accept and understand its invisible and nonphysical environment. But souls that are attached to their bodies and physical existence leave this world only with great reluctance. They may not have the discipline to follow their guides to the other world. There, they may be disoriented. Absorbed, as they are, in the affairs of the visible world, they may not comprehend their new invisible surroundings. They may then be forced to leave life and be dragged to the gath- ering point of the souls.

"'Where the souls migrate and meet each other, the souls

of the wicked who polluted and destroyed themselves by committing crimes and other unjust acts are ostracized by the other souls. One of the reasons it is better to suffer injustice than to commit it, is the effect committing an injustice has on the soul, which becomes apparent after death when souls are exposed to each other directly, without the mediation of the senses. Unjust souls that committed injustice are perceived directly by the other souls for what they are, with no ability to deceive as they do when they are perceived through the senses and behavior. Then they have no friends or guides to help direct them in the other world. They are lost in that "forest" of the other world, not knowing where to turn, forlorn and isolated. They wander from one place to another in utter confusion, until after a long time they stumble upon a place that is appropriate for them. By contrast, the philosophical and just souls are guided to their proper place, where they can converse with each other philosophically and come into direct contact with the pure ideas. This is what I believe.'

"'But do you know it? Can you prove this?' asked Simms. 'I have heard many stories and myths about death and what follows. But they are mutually inconsistent. Why should we believe one story rather than another? Your story seems original; at least, I have not heard anything similar. What is your reason for believing in it, or in the verbally inexpressible, indescribable reality you allude to by telling us this metaphorical myth?'

"For the first time in my long acquaintance with Socrates, he appeared somewhat impatient during a conversation.

"'Come on, Simms,' he said somewhat reproachfully. 'I told you I cannot prove any of it. Even if I could, there is no more time. Very soon it will be time for me to die and see for myself if I am right. I have no knowledge of what happens after death, only beliefs. Even if I did know it, I could not describe it in words. So just listen to my story and make the best of it. If it does not convince you, consider it a deathbed story, like the bedtime stories your parents may have told you when you were a boy.'

"Simms apologized politely for interrupting Socrates and asked him to continue with his story.

"'When the souls of the departed reach their gathering point, they must be judged. It is not clear to me if they are judged by each other or by some appointed judge. I do not know who that judge may be; he could be the guide who directs them there. Regardless, they are judged and then classified into four groups: the ones whose spirituality is balanced by their attachment to the body remain in the other world until they purify their souls of any physical contamination. They are punished for their misdeeds and rewarded for their good deeds. Then they can return to the world of the living and be reincarnated.

"'Souls that committed horrible crimes that corrupted them beyond any possibility of purification—murderers, for example—have the destiny of disappearing into a dark "vortex" from which they will never emerge. There will be no incarnation for them.

"'The damaged souls of unjust people who are judged to be curable, for example, souls that had been incapable of controlling their passions and desires and that committed crimes of passion—such as domestic violence or even hot-blooded murder—but that then spent their life regretting and trying to make amends for their crimes of passion, must be punished until they learn to bring their passions under the control of their reason. They must face the souls of their victims and beg for their forgiveness. If the victims accept their apologies as sincere and their reforming of their souls as real, these damaged souls can join the souls that purify themselves before being reincarnated. If those sinners do not convince their victims of the sincerity of their remorse, they go back into the vortex for more punishment before they try again to apologize to their victims. Only when the wronged victims accept the perpetrators back into the community of souls can these souls be released from the vortex and rejoin the cycle of rebirth and reincarnation.

"'Philosophers arrive in the afterworld ready, having fully controlled their bodily passions and desires and attuned in their mind's eye to the invisible ideas that inhabit that world. They require no further purification of the soul or of the remnants of the body. They can migrate directly to a pure world of clear ideas. That pure world is not like a forest with forking roads but is like a beautiful and sunny beach where sea and sky and earth are easily distinguished and every object is clear in the sun or as clear as the stars are on a cloudless summer night away from city lights. I imagine this place to be like the village of Pythagoreion on the Greek island of Samos, where I visited once a long time ago. There, the pure souls of the philosophers dwell among the perfect, absolute, and pure ideas, disembodied and with no desire to return to be incarnated in another body. There they are released from the cycle of reincarnation, embodiment, and death. They remain there living in truth, beauty, and justice.

"'As you can see, Simms, it is very difficult for me to describe in words a disembodied perfect world of ideas and souls. Even if I could, I have run out of time. My death is very near indeed. But I believe that the discussion we have had today concluded with sufficient reasons for leading a life in search and in service of wisdom and justice and truth. There is every reason to hope that attaining a just and wise soul is its own reward.

"'I admit that I have not given any reason to convince reasonable people of all the details of my mythical story. As a mythical story, it is not to be interpreted literally. Rational people may doubt the details: that after death the souls migrate; are led by a guide and then judged; are divided into four groups; and then—with the exception of the pure philosophers who remain with the ideas and the incurably wicked souls who are lost in a vortex—return to be reincarnated. But either this myth or something like it should be true. The prospects of existence after death, at least for a philosopher, are glorious. Whether or not the details resemble the story I have told you, it should suffice to comfort us as we embark on this journey to the other side of death. That is why I told this myth, though it is not a well-reasoned philosophical argument. It is a pleasant story about what may await us after we are dead. It should prepare us with joy and cheerfulness to accept death. A philosophical soul that separated itself from its body a long time ago and rejected its passions and pleasures, while following a life devoted to the love of and search for wisdom has already achieved in this life knowledge of the pure and perfect ideas. Such a soul has nothing to fear from death because it is already living in a manner quite similar to what may await it after the death of the body.

"'We live in a culture that takes great pains to avoid talking about death, thinking about death, accepting the inevitability of death. Talking about death, dying, or illness in public is as impolite as passing gas in public. Our society actively denies death. Consequently, people who live in ignorance and denial of death are not ready for it when, as sure as night follows day, it approaches, gets even nearer, and then comes. This denial has terrible effects on our lives here. How many people do you think would spend time watching wrestling, spend hours driving to find a slightly better deal on a purchase, or participate in sausage-eating competitions if they realized that one day—and that day may not be far off—they will die?! But we will all die: you, me, Simms and Sebastian, even young Apollo, some sooner and others later, but death is at the end of every-body from the richest banker to the poorest homeless, from the most powerful tyrant to the most powerless dissident, and everybody in between. Medieval artistic depictions of the danse macabre—the skeleton figure of death dancing with people from all walks of life—are good at reminding us that we will all die, everyone from the pope to the dandy, the king to the beggar. This medieval portrayal of death tends to be inter-preted as death being the great equalizer: no matter how high and mighty or low and humble we are, we will all die. This is true no matter the differences in class, wealth, and power. Rich people may live a bit longer than poor people, but they, too, will die in the end.

"'But there are other distinctions between people that do make a lot of difference when they face death. I have argued that philosophers who separate themselves from their bodies, passions, and physical attachments while they pursue wisdom and justice and abstract truth are better prepared to face death than people who live in denial of death and are attached to day-to-day concerns about their bodies, desires, consumption, production, and reproduction. As for me, my time is up, and I am ready. Destiny calls and I cannot put it on hold.'"

SOCRATES'S DEATH

"Chris, Socrates's oldest friend, who had been caring for him since they were teenagers, asked then whether Socrates had any last instructions or requests regarding his children or anything else his friends might perform as a last service.

"'Nothing special,' answered Socrates. 'Just do as I have always instructed you. Take good care of yourselves, care for

your souls. This is the best service you can give me and yourselves, whether or not you agree with what I have been saying.
By the same token, if you neglect your souls and fail to walk
on the path of life that I have recommended today and in the
countless other conversations we have had over the years, you
will be harming yourselves and me, no matter how much you
agree with me now.'

"Chris promised that we would do our best to take care
of our souls. He then asked Socrates how he would like to be
buried.

"'That is entirely up to you; you can bury my body in the
ground, cremate me, feed me to the animals at the zoo, or use
me for compost.' Socrates laughed and added, 'But if you want
to bury *me*, you will have to catch me first and then hold me so
I do not melt away. It is pretty difficult to catch a soul, and even
more difficult to hold it in one place.' Still smiling, he said,
'Good old Chris cannot believe that I have not died yet but am
still the same old Socrates who went to college with him and has
been talking the whole day. He addresses me as if I am a corpse,
asking me how I would like to be buried, even though I have
spent this whole day trying to explain that when this body dies,
I will not be here anymore but will migrate to another nonphysical, invisible world that will be far better suited for the philosophical pursuits than this one. Chris still thinks I am going to
die and be buried. Well, well, it seems like the strings of words
that came out of my mouth have had little effect on Chris. If he
does not pay attention to my assurances, perhaps you can help
me convince him that I will not remain in this body to die but
will leave this body and travel far away. If we manage to convince him of this, he will not suffer as much when I am dead
and will not be saddened when he sees my body being buried
or cremated or fed to the lions or whatever. I do not want him

to feel sorry for me or my bad luck. I certainly do not want him to say at my funeral that "Socrates lies here," or is being buried, or is being cremated. It is not going to be Socrates. It will be just what used to be Socrates's old and useless body. So, dear Chris, old friend, be a good chum, and when the time comes, say at the gravesite that you are burying my body and not me. You can do with my body whatever you see fit or whatever is traditional. Just be clear that there is nothing sacred about the body. The corpse is just a heap of dead meat, soon to start rotting. By then, the soul will be long gone.'

"Socrates asked the nurses to bathe him. He wanted to die clean. It symbolized both his faith in the purification of the soul and the more practical concern that nobody should have to wash his corpse after his death. Chris went with him to the bathroom while the rest of us waited. We talked and debated the topics Socrates covered in his discussion on that last day of his life. We also shared our profound sorrow. Socrates was more than a teacher or mentor to us. He was a kind of philosophical father whom we were sad to lose, knowing we would have to spend the rest of our lives as orphans.

"After Socrates had been bathed, his three sons and other relatives were allowed in. He bade them farewell and gave a few last practical instructions in the presence of Chris, who would assist in fulfilling those last requests. When they left, Socrates returned to us.

"Outside, the dawn broke. Socrates was sitting with us again, clean and smelling pleasant after his bath, but he was quiet. The doctor came in and stood next to his bed. He praised Socrates for being the gentlest and kindest patient he had ever had. Unlike other terminal patients, Socrates never felt anger or displayed rage at his fate. He always treated the doctors, nurses, and orderlies with the utmost respect and friendliness, without a hint of resentment. The doctor then set up the mechanism that would bring about the end of Socrates's life. When he was done, he could not contain himself any longer; he started crying, then quickly turned away and left Socrates's room.

"Socrates thanked him and wished him all the best for the rest of his life. He then told us how charming that doctor had been. 'He has been visiting me regularly; sometimes we discussed philosophical issues—he is particularly interested in medical ethics, in questions that have to do with the right or lack of a right to die, and the duty of a doctor to assist or the right of a doctor to withhold assistance. I think I pretty much convinced him in all my arguments. He treated me to the highest medical standards. Now, see how sorry he is to have to lose me and to assist me in my right to die. So, let's get on with it. Chris, can you please help me with this mechanism so I can switch it on, or should this button be called the switch-off button?'

"Chris said, 'Perhaps not so quickly. We can wait a while longer. Some people want to have a party, feast on the best food, drink the best wine, delight themselves with any sensual pleasure they think of, and only then die. I can send out for takeaway. We can then spend a little more time together.'

"Socrates laughed. 'Yes, dear Chris, the people who do all this partying before they die are right to do so from their perspective. They gain a little more time, squeeze a little more from the almost dry, bitter lemon of life. But I have nothing to gain from a delay of the inevitable. My life is at an end. It is over. I would feel ridiculous if I behaved in such a petty manner, attempting to bargain a few more minutes for life. Please do what I ask of you and do not make a fuss.'

"Obediently, Chris called the doctor back in. Socrates asked him to show him how to proceed. The doctor explained how to activate the machine that would end his life. Whatever sensations were left in his body would gradually disappear. He would become numb and relaxed until the chemicals from the machine reached his brain. Then he would lose consciousness and die. Socrates thanked him and, with an easy and gentle manner, with no fear or change of facial expression or tone of voice, looking at all of us directly as he always did, readily and cheerfully activated the machine. He wondered jokingly whether there was some sort of religious blessing that could be said over the procedure, like grace among the Christians or the blessing of the bread among the Jews. 'I must pray to all the gods of all the religions that my journey from this to the next world will be a successful and prosperous one. I hope this last wish is granted to me.'

"Until that point, most of us were able to hold back our emotions. But when we saw the machine beginning the irreversible process that would lead to the death of Socrates, we could not hold back any longer. Despite myself, my own tears started flowing. I covered my face with my hands to hide my tears and wept for my own sake, not for Socrates, at the thought of losing my friend, mentor, and teacher, of the utter loneliness that would await me. Chris, too, was overwhelmed.

"Then Apollo, who had been weeping all along, broke into a hysterical wail that resonated with all of us—except Socrates. Socrates remained entirely calm. 'What is this wailing for?' he asked. 'This is why I sent my family away. I did not want emotional outbursts. Death should take place in peace. Please, be quiet and be patient. It will not be long now.'

"Upon hearing this, we were ashamed of our emotional behavior and restrained ourselves. Socrates laid back, and the doctor touched his arms and legs, asking him if he could feel his limbs. Socrates could feel nothing. His body became cold and motionless. His eyes were closed. Then he suddenly opened them and said, 'Chris, I think I am finally cured. Somebody should recite a prayer to give thanks for it and make a donation.'

"'I will take care of it,' Chris assured him. 'Is there anything else?'

"Socrates did not reply. Those had been his last words. A moment or two later, the doctor pronounced him dead. Chris removed Socrates's hands from his face. His eyes were open and stared forward, but they were still. Chris gently closed his eyes and mouth.

"This is how our friend Socrates died, dear Cheryl. He was the wisest, the most just, and the best human being I have ever met and am likely to ever meet again in this life."

A FINAL INTERRUPTION

Cheryl wiped a tear from her eye. She sat there in silence with Fred for a few minutes, until suddenly they heard a voice from behind them saying, "Can I say something now?" They both recognized Simms immediately.

"Simms, what are you doing here in the middle of nowhere this late at night?" asked Fred.

"Here and now, I can finally talk freely and speak my mind. As long as the dialogue was going on and Socrates was alive, he could threaten me with expulsion from the dialogue if I did not follow his script. But now he is dead and the dialogue is finished. So let me tell you: I think he had a death wish. He just wanted to die. He considered life a sickness of the soul whose only cure is death. This is the meaning of his last words. He was already looking for a socially acceptable path to death when he refused Chris's offer to help him escape the country when he was conscripted to the military. In this dialogue he rejected suicide in principle, but he never explained why, except that it contravenes accepted social norms and that we are like live-stock belonging to God. This is hardly a reason for somebody as rational Socrates, who never respected common and traditional beliefs and norms. He usually gave bad arguments in favor of positions he pretended to accept but was actually opposed to. His argument for philosophical acceptance of death can very easily become an argument for suicide. In fact, it was. At least in some parts, this argument was very weak, especially the fairy tale he told at the end about the afterlife. He himself did not claim to have proved any of it. The theory of opposites in this visible world—not in the perfect world of eternal ideas—that says all opposites lead to each other and therefore life must come from death because death comes from life is so vague that it can be interpreted to fit all possible counterexamples simply by manipulating what we consider to be opposites.

"The value system Socrates endorses is radically antiphysical and antivisible. But is it the case that if we turn our attention away from what our eyes show us and our ears tell us that we will learn about truth and beauty? Empirical science infers truth from sense data. Without the beauty of nature and its sensual plea-sures, not much of what we consider beautiful remains. There is more to truth and beauty than abstract relationships. Anyway, what is so wrong about physical pleasure, love, and so on?! Must philosophers live in denial of their bodies? I am not sure.

"Socrates was right that we should not succumb to passions and desires and live in moderation and with self-control. People who give in to their fears and passions lead miserable lives, hurting themselves and others, being unjust not only to others but harming their own souls. Fear of death is particularly impor-tant because, as one of the strongest fears, it has been useful for manipulating people to do to themselves and others things that are worse than death. Socrates's attitude toward death, his fearlessness, calm, and composure have been exemplary. Combined with his long-held conviction that it is better to suffer injustice than to commit injustice because the commission of injustice destroys the soul that perpetrates it, his acceptance of death is an ongoing inspiration for political dissent, for philosophers telling truth to power, and for accepting the possible personal risks and consequences that follow a Socratic way of life.

"Socrates's philosophical discussion of death is a model for how philosophy can clarify issues that ordinary people are afraid of or are in denial about. This model can inspire people who hold unreflectively traditional beliefs about death and do not subject their beliefs to critical analysis. Socrates's highly abstract and ideal understanding of the soul and the world of absolute ideas where it should dwell after death marks intellectual progress in comparison with the physical and sensual characterizations of the soul and the afterlife in many traditional religions, which make the mistake of presuming that, even without a body or the five physical senses of sight, sound, smell, taste, and touch, the soul will continue to live the same kind of life it had on this earth, only with a higher standard of living. The theory of ideas, of independently existing absolute ideas that cannot change or become their opposites and that are reflected in our classifications and evaluations of everything we perceive through the senses solves some problems while creating many new ones. But this is not the place or the time to go into them."

Simms exhaled loudly and drank the glass of water Cheryl had given him. "Thank you, Cheryl. I needed to get that off my chest before this dialogue ends."

"Bravo, Simms," exclaimed Fred. "Feeling better?"

"Yes, much better. Thank you."

"You do not expect me to argue with you now, do you? I am not Socrates, and Socrates is dead and cannot reply to any of your criticisms. I am quite sure, though, that had he been with us, he would have answered you in great detail, and convincingly, too."

Simms acknowledged Fred's point. They spent a few more minutes reminiscing about Socrates. Then, recognizing that they had a long drive ahead of them, all three students of Socrates drove in three different directions into the cold night, still carrying with them a reflection of old Socrates to guide them through all the forks in the roads they must travel.

SUGGESTIONS FOR FURTHER READING

All of Plato's dialogues were translated into English. Benjamin Jowett's translations from the nineteenth century are the classical source I used in this adaptation. Penguin and other mass-market houses like Hackett have published more modern translations of selected dialogues, some with explanatory notes. The Loeb Classical Library has published bilingual editions of Plato's dialogues in the ancient Greek along with literal translations into English.

For secondary literature, I recommend the Blackwell Companions to Philosophy series, which comprises fifty volumes that cover all the main subfields of philosophy. Of particular interest are the following titles.

Ahbel-Rappe, Sara, and Rachana Kamtekar, eds. *A Companion to Socrates.* Boston: Wiley-Blackwell, 2009.

Benson, Hugh H., ed. *A Companion to Plato.* Boston: Wiley-Blackwell, 2009.

Fine, Gail, ed. *The Oxford Handbook to Plato.* New York: Oxford University Press, 2011.

Kraut, Richard, ed. *The Cambridge Companion to Plato.* New York: Cambridge University Press, 1992.

Morrison, Donald R., ed. *The Cambridge Companion to Socrates.* New York: Cambridge University Press, 2010.

Each of these companions and handbooks contains dozens of articles by recognized authorities about various aspects of the philosophies of Socrates and Plato with extensive bibliographies.

For contemporary uses of the philosophy of Plato that demonstrate its relevance for everybody, I recommend the following.

Marinoff, Lou. *Plato, Not Prozac! Applying Eternal Wisdom to Everyday Problems.* New York: HarperCollins, 1999. Marinoff, following Socrates, questions the expertise of psychotherapists and proposes philosophy instead.

Patočka, Jan. *Plato and Europe.* Translated by Petr Lom. Stanford, CA: Stanford University Press, 2002. This book by the Czech dissident leader and founder of the Charter 77 movement for human rights demonstrates how Socrates's practice and Plato's philosophy were able to form a philosophical foundation for an antitotalitarian dissident movement bent on Socratic care for the soul and life in truth.